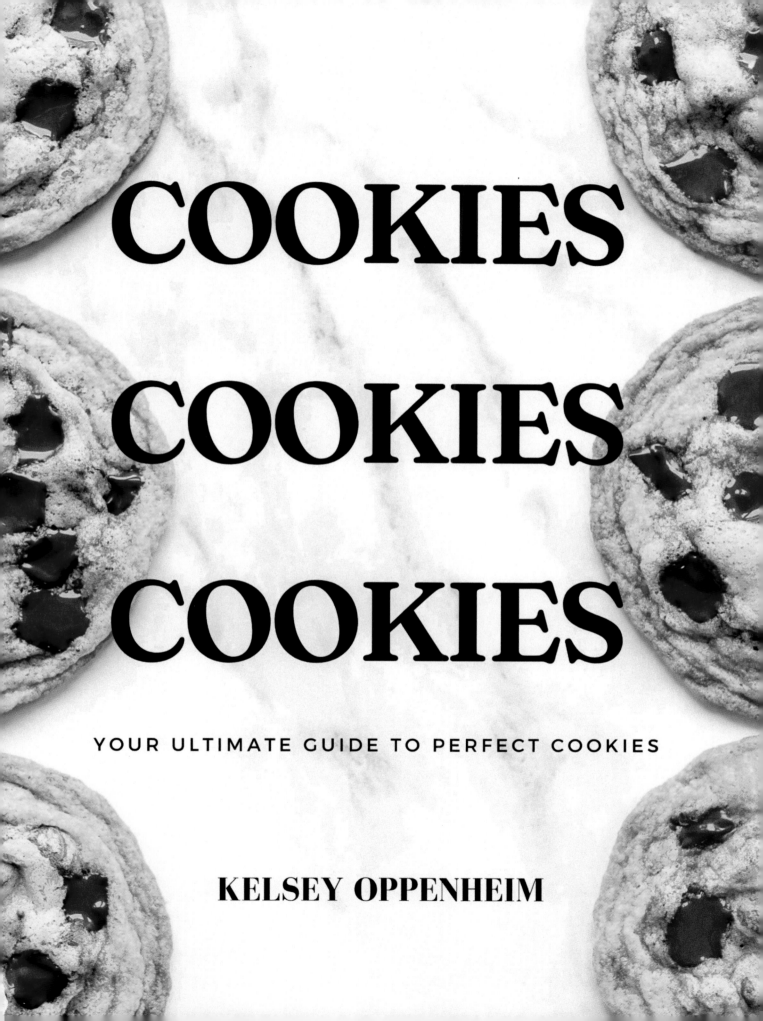

COOKIES COOKIES COOKIES

YOUR ULTIMATE GUIDE TO PERFECT COOKIES

KELSEY OPPENHEIM

To my Mom,
who has a heart sweeter
than the perfect chocolate chip cookie.

CONTENTS

INTRODUCTION

Cookies have always been a special part of my life. Some of my sweetest memories are wrapped up in the smells of vanilla, chocolate, and sugar wafting through the kitchen. I can still picture myself as a little girl, standing on tiptoes at the counter with my mom and sister, mixing up a box of brownies and taking turns stirring the batter. I remember the warmth of fresh chocolate chip cookies waiting for me after the first day of school, paired with a tall glass of cold milk while we talked about our day. And I'll never forget the magical baking days with my grandparents every holiday season, where we'd spend hours in the kitchen making the classic cookies they grew up with, all to the sound of Christmas music playing in the background. These moments are part of what made my childhood so sweet, and they've inspired me to share that magic with you through this cookie cookbook. Because if there's one thing I believe, it's that everyone deserves a little sweetness in their life. Cookies have this incredible ability to turn the ordinary into something special. Whether you're whipping up a batch for a celebration or just treating yourself on a quiet afternoon, they make everything feel a little brighter. As you bake your way through these pages, I hope you create your own memories— whether it's with loved ones, or simply taking a moment for yourself. This cookbook is my love letter to those cherished times in the kitchen, and I hope it brings the same warmth and joy to your home that it has to mine. Let's make life a little sweeter, one cookie at a time.

INGREDIENTS 101

By understanding how these key ingredients work, you can perfect your cookies' flavor, texture, and appearance, achieving the results you want every time.

FLOUR is the backbone of most cookies, providing structure and texture. The way you measure it matters a lot—spooning and leveling flour ensures you don't pack too much into your measuring cup, which can lead to dense or dry cookies. Cake flour is finer and has less protein, making cookies lighter and more tender, while all-purpose flour is a reliable choice for structure. Too much flour, or the wrong type, can leave you with a tough or crumbly cookie.

BUTTER adds flavor and helps create the perfect cookie texture, but its temperature makes a big difference. Softened butter, which holds its shape but indents when pressed, is perfect for creaming with sugar, giving cookies a tender crumb. Room temperature butter blends easily but won't hold air as well, resulting in denser cookies. Cold butter is ideal for recipes where you want to prevent too much spreading. Unsalted butter gives you control over the salt in the recipe, while salted butter can add a slight but noticeable difference in flavor.

EGGS bind the dough and add moisture, contributing to both texture and structure. The size of your egg matters—a large egg is the standard for most recipes, and using a different size could throw off the liquid-to-dry ingredient ratio. Egg temperature is important too—room temperature eggs blend more smoothly into dough, helping create a more even texture, while cold eggs can result in uneven mixing, affecting how your cookies bake.

GRANULATED SUGAR gives cookies a crisp edge and helps with spreading, while **LIGHT BROWN SUGAR**, which contains molasses, adds a bit of chewiness and moisture. **DARK BROWN SUGAR** has even more molasses, creating a deeper flavor and an extra chewy texture. The balance between these sugars affects both the flavor and texture of your cookies, giving you control over how crispy, chewy, or moist they turn out.

COCOA POWDER is acidic and reacts with baking soda to help cookies rise. **DUTCH-PROCESSED COCOA**, on the other hand, is alkalized, which neutralizes the acid and gives it a deeper, richer chocolate flavor. Using Dutch-processed cocoa will result in a slightly darker, smoother-tasting cookie, while regular cocoa adds a sharper chocolate note and more rise if combined with baking soda.

VANILLA extract or vanilla bean paste is crucial in cookies because it enhances the flavor profile, adding depth and warmth. Even though it might seem like a small amount, vanilla brings out the sweetness of the other ingredients and rounds out the overall taste, giving cookies that classic, comforting flavor. Vanilla bean paste, with its concentrated flavor and visible specks of vanilla, adds an even richer, more intense taste, making cookies taste gourmet. Skipping it can leave your cookies tasting flat or incomplete.

BAKING POWDER & BAKING SODA are leavening agents and give cookies lift. Baking soda is a base that requires an acid (like brown sugar or cocoa powder) to activate, making cookies spread more and become crisp. Baking powder, on the other hand, contains both an acid and a base, allowing it to act as a double agent, helping cookies rise without relying on other ingredients. The right balance of both ensures cookies are light, airy, and perfectly textured.

KOSHER SALT is just as important as sugar when it comes to cookies. It helps balance the sweetness and enhances the flavor of all the other ingredients. Without salt, cookies can taste overly sweet or one-dimensional. Kosher salt, with its coarser texture, distributes more evenly in dough and gives a subtler saltiness than table salt, which can sometimes taste too sharp. The right amount of salt brings out the best in your cookies, elevating their flavor to a more complex, satisfying level.

COOKIE JAR FAVORITES

THE PERFECT CHOCOLATE CHIP COOKIES

No one complains about a chocolate chip cookie for dessert. Whenever I bring something over to a friend's house to share, these chocolate chip cookies are my go-to. I have tried a lot of chocolate chip cookies in my time and would consider myself a bit of a cookie expert, so trust me when I say these chocolate chip cookies are the best in the world. They have the perfect combination of crispy edges and a gooey, soft center that melts in your mouth. The buttery dough is rich, the chocolate chips are perfectly melted, and the hint of vanilla adds just the right warmth. Plus, a sprinkle of sea salt on top makes them absolutely irresistible. Everyone needs a perfect chocolate chip cookie recipe in their collection, and this will be your go-to forever. You can brown the butter, add milk chocolate, and a sprinkle of flaky sea salt to make these even more delicious! This is the perfect chocolate chip cookie, and everyone will be begging you for your recipe.

1¼ cups (160g) all-purpose flour, spooned and leveled

½ teaspoon baking soda

½ teaspoon kosher salt

½ cup (113g) unsalted butter, softened

½ cup (105g) light brown sugar, packed

¼ cup (50g) granulated sugar

½ teaspoon vanilla extract

1 large egg, room temperature

1 cup (170g) semi-sweet chocolate chips

Flaky sea salt for topping, if desired

1 Preheat the oven to 350°F (175°C) and line two baking sheets with parchment paper.

2 In a medium bowl, whisk together the all-purpose flour, baking soda, and salt. Set this aside.

3 In a large mixing bowl, beat together the softened butter, brown sugar, and granulated sugar. Mix until smooth and creamy. Add the vanilla extract and egg and mix until well combined on medium speed. Gradually mix the dry ingredients into the wet mixture until just combined. Be careful not to overmix. Using a rubber spatula, fold in the chocolate chips.

4 Using a 3-tablespoon sized cookie dough scoop, scoop out the dough into balls and place them on the prepared baking sheet. Bake for 10-12 minutes, or until the edges are golden but the centers are still soft. Allow the cookies to cool on the baking sheet for 5 minutes before transferring them to a wire rack to cool completely. Sprinkle with flaky sea salt if desired.

DROP STYLE CHEWY SUGAR COOKIES

MAKES 14 COOKIES

Chewy, sweet sugar cookies are absolutely irresistible. With a soft and buttery texture, these cookies are elevated by the subtle, nutty flavor of almond, making each bite absolutely delicious. Yes! You can substitute the almond extract for more vanilla. Perfect for any occasion, these cookies are easy to make and sure to become a favorite in your recipe collection.

2¾ cups (330g) all-purpose flour, spooned and leveled

1 teaspoon baking soda

½ teaspoon baking powder

½ teaspoon kosher salt

1 cup (227g) unsalted butter, softened

1 cup (200g) granulated sugar, plus ½ cup (100g) more for rolling

½ cup (105g) light brown sugar, packed

1 large egg, room temperature

1 egg yolk, room temperature

½ teaspoon almond extract

1 teaspoon vanilla extract

⅛ cup (25g) sparkling sugar for topping

1 Whisk together the all-purpose flour, baking soda, baking powder, and salt in a bowl and set it aside.

2 In a large bowl, beat together the butter, granulated sugar, and brown sugar until it's light and fluffy, about 2 minutes. Add in the egg and egg yolk one at a time followed by the almond and vanilla extract until fully incorporated. Slowly add in the dry ingredients until a dough forms. Do not overmix.

3 Allow the dough to chill in the fridge for 30 minutes. During the last 15 minutes of chill time, preheat the oven to 350°F (175°C) and line two baking sheets with parchment paper.

4 Using a 3 tbsp sized cookie dough scoop, scoop out the dough, roll them in sugar, place them on the baking sheets, and bake for 9-11 minutes. Let the cookies cool on the baking sheet before transferring them to a cooling rack. Sprinkle the cookies with sparkling sugar.

PEANUT BUTTER COOKIES

MAKES 12 COOKIES

These chewy peanut butter cookies are pure perfection. Each bite is soft and rich, with a deep, nutty flavor that melts in your mouth. The texture is irresistibly chewy, with just the right balance of sweetness from honey and the bold taste of peanut butter. If you're a peanut butter lover, this cookie is everything you've been craving—comforting, indulgent, and impossible to have just one!

1 cup (120g) all-purpose flour, spooned and leveled

½ teaspoon baking soda

½ teaspoon baking powder

¼ teaspoon kosher salt

½ cup (113g) unsalted butter, softened

¾ cup (160g) light brown sugar, packed

¼ cup (50g) granulated sugar

1 large egg, room temperature

1 egg yolk, room temperature

1½ teaspoon vanilla extract

⅓ cup creamy peanut butter, like Jif

1 tablespoon honey

1   Preheat the oven to 350°F (175°C) and line two baking sheets with parchment paper.

2   In a medium bowl, whisk together the flour, baking soda, baking powder, and salt. Set this aside.

3   In a large bowl, cream together the butter, brown sugar, and granulated sugar for 2 minutes until creamy and light. Add in the egg, egg yolk, and vanilla and mix for an additional 2 minutes until fluffy. Add the peanut butter and honey and mix until combined. Sprinkle in the dry ingredients and mix until just combined, there will be some streaks.

4   Scoop out 3 tbsp sized balls of cookie dough and place on the parchment lined baking sheets 2 inches apart to allow for spreading. Bake for 8-10 minutes, until the edges are just slightly darker than the center of the cookie. Allow the cookies to cool on the baking sheet for a few minutes before transferring them to a wire rack to continue cooling.

DOUBLE FUDGY CHOCOLATE COOKIES

MAKES 10 COOKIES

These fudgy chocolate cookies loaded with melty chocolate chips are a chocolate lover's DREAM. They are rich and decadent double chocolate cookies with a soft and chewy center and a slightly crisp exterior. Get a glass of cold milk ready, they are best enjoyed freshly warm out of the oven dunked right in.

1⅓ cups (160g) all-purpose flour, spooned and leveled

⅓ cup (28g) Dutch processed cocoa powder

½ teaspoon baking soda

¼ teaspoon kosher salt

½ cup (113g) unsalted butter, softened

½ cup (105g) light brown sugar, packed

⅓ cup (67g) granulated sugar

1 large egg, room temperature

1 teaspoon vanilla extract

¾ cup (113g) semi-sweet chocolate chips, plus more for topping

1   Preheat the oven to 350°F (175°C) and line two baking sheets with parchment paper.

2   In a medium bowl, whisk together the all-purpose flour, cocoa powder, baking soda, and salt. Set this aside.

3   In a large mixing bowl, beat together the butter, brown sugar, and granulated sugar until light and fluffy, about 2 minutes. Add in the egg and vanilla and mix until combined. Sprinkle in the dry ingredients and mix on low until just combined. Be careful not to overmix. Using a rubber spatula, fold in the semi-sweet chocolate chips.

4   Using a 3 tbsp sized cookie dough scoop, scoop out the cookies and place them on the prepared baking sheets. Bake 6 cookies at a time for 9-12 minutes. Once the cookies are done baking, gently swirl a round cookie cutter around the border of the cookie to form it back into a perfect circle. Top the cookies with extra chocolate chips if desired.

MINI M&M COOKIES

MAKES 24 COOKIES

Growing up, there was this little market that sold mini M&M cookies, and they were my absolute favorite. I could eat a whole container in one sitting, they were that good! There's something about the mini M&Ms that makes them even better—each bite is packed with just the right amount of chocolate crunch and sweetness. These cookies are soft and chewy, with colorful mini candies in every bite, giving them the perfect pop of texture and flavor. Trust me, they have to be mini!

1⅓ cups (160g) all-purpose flour, spooned and leveled

½ teaspoon baking soda

½ teaspoon baking powder

½ teaspoon kosher salt

½ cup (113g) unsalted butter, softened

½ cup (105g) light brown sugar, packed

⅓ cup (67g) granulated sugar

1 large egg, room temperature

1 teaspoon vanilla extract

1 cup (224g) mini semi-sweet chocolate chips

½ cup (100g) mini M&M's, plus more for topping if desired

1 Preheat the oven to 350°F (175°C) and line two baking sheets with parchment paper.

2 In a medium bowl, whisk together the flour, baking soda, baking powder, and salt. Set this aside.

3 In a large bowl, beat together the butter, brown sugar, and granulated sugar on high until smooth and creamy, about 2 minutes. Scrape down the sides of the bowl. Reduce the speed to medium low and add in the egg and vanilla and mix until combined. Sprinkle in the dry ingredients and mix until just combined, but streaks remain. Using a rubber spatula, fold the mini chocolate chips and mini M&M's into the dough.

4 Using a 1 tbsp sized cookie dough scoop, scoop out 24 cookie dough balls and place them on the prepared baking sheets with 2 inches in between each one. Bake for 7-9 minutes until the edges just start to turn slightly golden. For a perfect circle shaped cookie, use a cookie cutter that's just slightly larger than the cookie, and while still slightly warm, wiggle the cookie cutter around the cookie, smoothing out the shape. Top with additional mini M&M's.

BUTTERY SHORTBREAD

MAKES 24 SHORTBREAD COOKIES

Everyone needs a classic, buttery shortbread recipe in their recipe box. Don't worry! These are not your average dry, crumbly shortbread. They're speckled with real flecks of vanilla bean and rich butter, making each bite melt in your mouth. These comforting shortbread cookies are the perfect treat to enjoy with your warm mug of tea and sugar or to include in your holiday cookie box.

½ cup (113g) unsalted butter, softened

½ cup (60g) powdered sugar

½ teaspoon vanilla bean paste or extract

1¼ cups (180g) all-purpose flour

¼ teaspoon kosher salt

1   In a large mixing bowl, beat the softened butter and powdered sugar together until light and fluffy, about 2-3 minutes. Mix in the vanilla bean paste or extract on medium speed until fully incorporated. Gradually add the flour and salt to the butter mixture, mixing just until combined. Be careful not to overmix so the cookies do not become tough and dry.

2   Form the dough into a disk, wrap it tightly in plastic wrap, and refrigerate for at least 30 minutes to an hour. During the last 15 minutes of chill time, preheat the oven to 350°F (175°C) and line two baking sheets with parchment paper.

3   Roll out the dough on a lightly floured surface to about ¼-inch thick. Use a cookie cutter to cut out shapes. Place the cookies on the prepared baking sheet and bake for 9-11 minutes, or until the edges are just turning golden. Let the cookies cool on the baking sheet for 5 minutes before transferring them to a wire rack. Dust with powdered sugar, if desired.

CHEWY BROWN BUTTER SNICKERDOODLES

MAKES 12 COOKIES

Snickerdoodles are a universal favorite cookie, so it is important that you have the absolute best recipe in your recipe box! Out of all the cookies in this cookbook, I tested these snickerdoodle cookies the most. They had to be absolutely perfect! The brown butter gives them the most incredible, nutty flavor and the perfect chew. They are soft with a slight sugary crunch from the cinnamon sugar. Completely irresistible, this will be your go-to snickerdoodle recipe forever and ever.

FOR THE COOKIES

1 cup (226g) unsalted butter, browned

2¾ cups (330g) all-purpose flour

½ teaspoon baking soda

½ teaspoon baking powder

1 teaspoon cream of tartar

1 tablespoon cornstarch

½ teaspoon kosher salt

1 teaspoon ground cinnamon

¾ cup (150g) granulated sugar

½ cup (106g) light brown sugar

1 egg, room temperature

1 egg yolk, room temperature

1 teaspoon vanilla extract

FOR THE ROLLING

¼ cup (50g) granulated sugar

1 tablespoon cinnamon

1 Preheat the oven to 350°F (175°C) and line two baking sheets with parchment paper.

2 Start by browning the butter. In a saucepan over medium heat, melt the butter. Continue cooking, stirring often, until the butter turns golden brown with a nutty aroma, about 5-10 minutes. Remove from heat and let it cool completely.

3 In a medium bowl, whisk together the flour, baking soda, baking powder, cream of tartar, cornstarch, salt, and cinnamon. Set this aside.

4 In a large mixing bowl, beat together the completely cooled brown butter, granulated sugar, and brown sugar on high until fully combined and forms a paste like texture. Add the egg, egg yolk, and vanilla and mix on medium until incorporated. Gradually add the dry ingredients to the wet mixture and mix until just combined. In a small bowl, mix together the granulated sugar and cinnamon for rolling.

5 Using a 3 tbsp sized cookie dough scoop, scoop out dough balls, roll them in the cinnamon sugar, and place on the prepared baking sheets. Bake for 9-11 minutes. Allow the cookies to cool completely before serving! Top with additional cinnamon sugar if desired.

SPRINKLE FUNFHETTI COOKIES

MAKES 14 COOKIES

Have you ever seen anything more festive and colorful than rainbow Funfetti sprinkle cookies? They're buttery, sugary, and packed full of beautiful rainbow sprinkles. These slightly crunchy and chewy sprinkle cookies are the perfect cookie for any celebration!

1⅓ cups (160g) all-purpose flour, spooned and leveled

1 teaspoon cornstarch

½ teaspoon baking soda

¼ teaspoon kosher salt

½ cup (113g) unsalted butter, softened

½ cup (100g) granulated sugar

¼ cup (53g) light brown sugar, packed

1 large egg yolk, room temperature

1 teaspoon vanilla extract

½ cups (80g) rainbow sprinkles, plus more for rolling

1   Preheat the oven to 350°F (175°C) and line two baking sheets with parchment paper.

2   In a medium bowl, whisk together the all-purpose flour, cornstarch, baking soda, and salt. Set this aside.

3   In a large mixing bowl, beat together the butter, granulated sugar, and brown sugar on high until light and creamy, about two minutes.

4   Mix in the egg yolk and vanilla extract on medium speed until combined. Sprinkle in the dry ingredients and mix on low until just combined. Fold in the sprinkles. Add some extra sprinkles to a small bowl for rolling the dough if desired.

5   Scoop out 2 tablespoon size cookie dough balls and roll the tops of the cookie dough balls in the extra sprinkles. Place the cookie dough on the prepared baking sheets and bake for 8 -10 minutes. Allow the cookies to sit on the baking tray for a few minutes before transferring them to a wire cooling rack to finish cooling completely.

RED VELVET COOKIES

MAKES 12 COOKIES

Red velvet cookies are just as delicious as they are beautiful. With their vibrant hue, each bite is packed with chocolatey, cocoa goodness. These red velvet cookies are delicious on their own, and you can also add your own mix-ins whether that's white chocolate or milk chocolate chips or frosting on top! Enjoy these year round, or for a festive holiday treat. I've heard they may just be Santa's favorite!

1½ cups (180g) all-purpose flour, spooned and leveled

1 tablespoon (10g) Dutch processed cocoa powder

½ teaspoon baking soda

½ teaspoon baking powder

½ teaspoon kosher salt

¾ cup (170g) unsalted butter, softened

¾ cup (160g) light brown sugar, packed

¼ cup (50g) granulated sugar

2 egg yolks, room temperature

1½ teaspoons vanilla extract

2 teaspoons red gel food coloring

1   Preheat the oven to 350°F (175°C) and line two baking sheets with parchment paper. In a medium bowl, whisk together the flour, cocoa powder, baking soda, baking powder, and salt. Set this aside.

2   In a large mixing bowl, beat together the butter, brown sugar, and granulated sugar on high until light and fluffy, about two minutes. Reduce the speed to medium and add in the egg yolks one at a time until mixed in. Add the vanilla extract and red gel food coloring and mix until combined. Sprinkle in the dry ingredients and mix on low until just combined. Be careful not to overmix.

3   Using a 3 tbsp sized scoop, scoop out cookie dough balls and place them 2 inches apart on the prepared baking sheets. Bake for 8-10 minutes. Allow the cookies to cool on the baking sheets for 2 minutes before transferring to a wire cooling rack.

CHEWY THICK OATMEAL RAISIN COOKIES

MAKES 12 COOKIES

Chewy oatmeal raisin cookies are such a nostalgic treat for me. Whether you're excited or a little disappointed to discover that a cookie has raisins instead of chocolate chips, these cookies will win you over. There's something so comforting about the combination of hearty oats and sweet, plump raisins that takes me back to my childhood. The hint of cinnamon adds warmth, making them the perfect cookie for cozy afternoons with a glass of cold milk. No matter how many cookies I try, these will always hold a special place in my heart—and they might just become your favorite, too!

¾ cup (90g) all-purpose flour, spooned and leveled

½ teaspoon baking soda

½ teaspoon ground cinnamon

⅛ teaspoon kosher salt

1½ cups (135g) old-fashioned rolled oats

½ cup (113g) unsalted butter, softened

6 tablespoons (75g) light brown sugar, packed

¼ cup (50g) granulated sugar

1 large egg, room temperature

½ teaspoon vanilla extract

½ cup (75g) raisins

1 Preheat the oven to 350°F (175°C) and line two baking sheets with parchment paper.

2 In a medium bowl, whisk together the all-purpose flour, baking soda, cinnamon, salt, and old-fashioned oats. Set this aside. Beat together the butter, brown sugar, and granulated sugar on high until light and creamy, about 2 minutes. Add in the egg and vanilla and mix on medium speed until fully incorporated. Mix in the dry ingredients on low until just combined. Fold in the raisins using a rubber spatula.

3 Scoop out 3 tablespoons of dough and place them on the prepared baking sheets leaving 2 inches between each cookie. Bake for 9-11 minutes, or until the edges are golden brown, but the centers look slightly under done. Let the cookies cool on the baking sheet for 5 minutes before transferring them to a wire rack to cool completely.

CUT OUT SUGAR COOKIES

MAKES 12 MEDIUM COOKIES

Every year during the holiday season, we put on a Christmas movie, bake a big batch of these cut out sugar cookies to decorate while Christmas cheer fills the room. Classic cut-out sugar cookies are a must-have for every season! They're so much fun to make in any shape —perfect for adding a festive touch to any occasion. Whether you're making holiday-themed cookies for Christmas or cute heart-shaped ones for Valentine's Day, these cookies are always a hit. They are also one of my favorite cookies to gift! For Thanksgiving, I make these sugar cookies into Turkeys and frost everyone's names on them as their place setting. What a fun treat for your guest to bring home at the end of the evening! They have a soft, buttery texture and a sweet, vanilla flavor that pairs perfectly with colorful icing and sprinkles. They're as fun to decorate as they are to eat!

2⅓ cups (280g) all-purpose flour, spooned and leveled, plus more for rolling out the dough

½ teaspoon baking powder

½ teaspoon kosher salt

¾ cup (170g) unsalted butter, softened

¾ cup (150g) granulated sugar

1 large egg, room temperature

2 teaspoons vanilla extract

1½ teaspoons almond extract

1   In a medium bowl, whisk together the all-purpose flour, baking powder, and salt. Set this aside. In a large mixing bowl, beat together the butter and sugar until it is light and fluffy, about 2 minutes. Add in the egg, vanilla, and almond extract mixing on medium until incorporated. Scrape down the sides as you mix. Sprinkle in the dry ingredients and mix on low until just combined.

2   On a lightly floured parchment paper, roll the dough out with a lightly floured rolling pin to about ¼" thickness. Cover the dough with plastic wrap and place it in the fridge to chill for at least 1 hour. During the last 15 minutes of chill time, preheat the oven to 350°F (175°C) and line two baking sheets with parchment paper.

3   Take the dough out of the refrigerator and use any cookie cutter shape you desire to cut out cookies. Re-roll the leftover dough and continue cutting out cookies. Place the cookies on the prepared baking sheets 2 inches apart and bake for 9-11 minutes. Turn the tray around in the oven halfway through the baking time. Allow the cookies to fully cool before decorating.

ROYAL ICING

MAKES ICING FOR 12 LARGE COOKIES

Royal icing is the secret to beautifully decorated cookies that look as good as they taste. With just powdered sugar, a bit of water, and meringue powder, this icing dries to a smooth, firm finish, making it perfect for detailed designs, lettering, or giving cookies a shiny, picture-perfect coating. Whether you're outlining, flooding, or adding delicate patterns, royal icing lets you get creative and keeps your decorations looking crisp. It's ideal for making your holiday cookies, gingerbread houses, and special treats feel a little more magical and impressive!

4 cups powdered sugar, sifted

3 tablespoons meringue powder

½ teaspoon vanilla extract

½ teaspoon almond extract

⅓ cup water, plus more for flood icing

1-3 drops gel food coloring, color of your choice

1   Add all the ingredients to a mixing bowl of a stand mixer. Using a whisk attachment, mix on low until combined.

2   Increase the speed to medium high and mix for 3-4 minutes until the icing is thick and shiny. The peaks of the icing should stand up straight without falling over. This icing will be used for the border of the cookies.

3   If you are making several different colors, divide the icing into different bowls and mix in the gel food coloring with a rubber spatula. Add the icing to a piping bag, cut the tip off at the very end of the bag, and pipe the border onto each cookie. Make sure not to let the piping bag touch the cookie, hover it just above as you pipe the border. This will give you more control over where the icing is falling.

4   After the border has set, add a little more water to each color icing you're using (½ tsp at a time) until it is slightly thinner and more spreadable. This is your flood icing.

5   Add a spoonful of the flood icing to the center of the cookie and use a toothpick to bring it all the way to the border. Allow the icing to set before serving.

WHITE CHOCOLATE MACADAMIA NUT COOKIES

MAKES 16 COOKIES

I absolutely fell in love with macadamia on our honeymoon to Hawaii! Each morning, with a macadamia nut latte in hand, we would walk the beach at sunrise. Crunchy macadamia nuts paired with creamy and sweet white chocolate make for a heavenly combination that will transport you to a vacation at any time.

2¾ cups (330g) all-purpose flour, spooned and leveled

1 teaspoon baking soda

½ teaspoon baking powder

½ teaspoon kosher salt

1 cup (227g) unsalted butter, softened

1 cup (200g) granulated sugar

½ cup (105g) light brown sugar, packed

1 large egg, room temperature

1 egg yolk, room temperature

1½ teaspoons vanilla extract

1 cup white chocolate chips

½ cup macadamia nuts, chopped

1   Preheat the oven to 350°F (175°C) and line two baking sheets with parchment paper.

2   Whisk together the flour, baking soda, baking powder, and salt in a bowl. Set this aside.

3   In a large mixing bowl, beat the butter, granulated sugar, and brown sugar on high until it's light and fluffy. About 2 minutes. Add in the egg and egg yolk one at a time followed by the vanilla until fully incorporated. Slowly add and mix in the dry ingredients until a dough forms. Do not overmix. Using a rubber spatula, fold in the white chocolate chips and chopped macadamia nuts.

4   Using a 3 tbsp sized cookie dough scoop, scoop out cookie dough balls, place them on the baking sheets, and bake for 9-11 minutes. Let the cookies cool on the baking sheet before transferring them to a cooling rack.

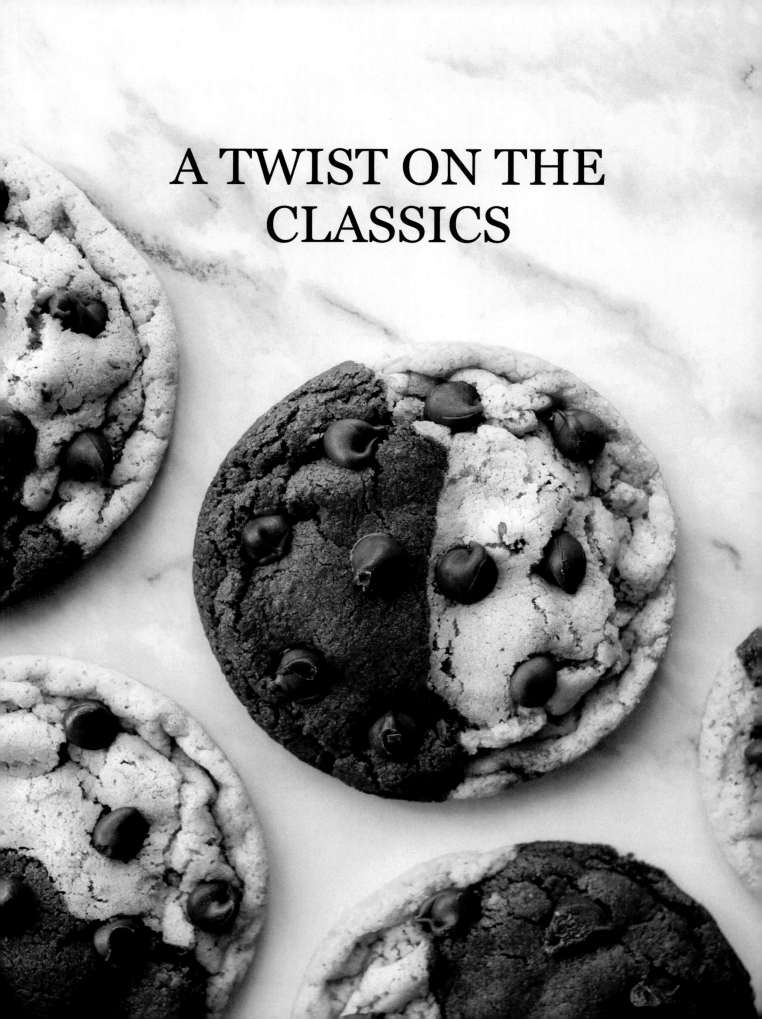

A TWIST ON THE CLASSICS

BAKERY STYLE CHOCOLATE CHIP COOKIES

MAKES 8 LARGE COOKIES

Number one reason I am hopping on a plane for a trip to NYC? I have to confess, it's chocolate chip cookies! Super thick bakery-style chocolate chip cookies are a chocolate lover's dream come true. These cookies are soft and gooey on the inside, with a perfectly crisp edge that makes each bite heavenly. Stuffed with a generous mix of milk chocolate, semi-sweet chocolate, and mini semi-sweet chips, they're not lacking on chocolate. Topped with a sprinkle of flaky sea salt, the sweet and salty combination takes these cookies to another level of deliciousness. These are the perfect, humongous cookies to gift to all your friends and family.

2½ cups (300g) cake flour, sifted

1½ teaspoons baking powder

1 teaspoon baking soda

¾ teaspoon kosher salt

½ cup (113g) unsalted butter, softened

1 cup (210g) light brown sugar, packed

¼ (50g) cup granulated sugar

2 eggs, room temperature

1 tsp vanilla extract

1 cup (170g) semi-sweet chocolate chips

1½ cups (255g) mini semi-sweet chocolate chips, divided

1 cup (170g) milk chocolate chips

Flaky sea salt, for topping

1   In a medium bowl, whisk together the sifted cake flour, baking powder, baking soda, and salt. Set this aside. In a large mixing bowl, beat together the butter, brown sugar, and granulated sugar until smooth and creamy, about 2 minutes. Add one egg at a time, mixing on medium low until fully incorporated followed by the vanilla. Sprinkle in the dry ingredients and mix until just combined. Fold in the semi-sweet chocolate chips, mini semi-sweet chocolate chips (save ½ cup for rolling), and milk chocolate chips.

2   Scoop out 5oz of cookie dough and roughly roll them into balls. Roll the tops and sides in the remaining mini semi-sweet chocolate chips (avoid the bottom so the chocolate does not burn). The dough will be slightly sticky so wash your hands in between rolling each cookie dough ball. Place all 8 cookie dough balls on a parchment paper lined baking sheet, and transfer to the refrigerator to chill for 1 hour. During the last 15 minutes of chill time, preheat the oven to 375°F (190°C) and line a second baking sheet with parchment paper. Place 4 cookie dough balls on each baking sheet (you can re-roll them slightly if needed as the dough will be easier to work with).

3   Bake for 11-15 minutes. Start watching the cookies at the 10-minute mark. They are done when the tops become golden brown. Allow the cookies to set on the baking sheet for at least 20 minutes. They will continue baking and setting as they cool. Top with flaky sea salt and enjoy.

THICK AND CHEWY FROSTED SUGAR COOKIES

MAKES 12 COOKIES

Thick and chewy sugar cookies topped with a layer of sweet, almond buttercream are in my top 3 favorite cookies of all time. These sugar cookies are so special with a perfectly soft and cakey texture that comes from a secret ingredient, powdered sugar. Topped with a luscious layer of creamy almond buttercream, each bite is a delightful blend of sweetness and nuttiness. Perfect for special occasions or a sweet treat any day, these cookies are sure to impress and quickly become a beloved favorite.

FOR THE COOKIES

1½ cups (180g) all-purpose flour

¼ teaspoon salt

¾ teaspoon baking powder

¼ teaspoon baking soda

½ cup (113g) unsalted butter, softened

⅓ cup (67g) granulated sugar

3 tablespoons (23g) powdered sugar

1 large egg, room temperature

½ teaspoon vanilla extract

½ teaspoon almond extract

FOR THE BUTTERCREAM

½ cup (113g) unsalted butter, softened

2½ cups (300g) powdered sugar

¾ teaspoon almond extract

½ teaspoon vanilla extract

1-3 tablespoons heavy cream

Sprinkles for topping, if desired

1 Preheat the oven to 350°F (175°C) and line two baking sheets with parchment paper. In a medium bowl, whisk together the flour, salt, baking powder, and baking soda. Set this aside.

2 In a large mixing bowl, beat together the butter, granulated sugar, and powdered sugar until light and fluffy, about 2 minutes. Add in the egg, vanilla, and almond extract mixing on medium speed until fully combined. Sprinkle in the dry ingredients and mix on low until just combined. Do not overmix.

3 Use a 2-tablespoon sized cookie dough scoop to scoop out the cookie dough. Roll it between your hand to form a circle, place it on the prepared baking sheets, and press down to slightly flatten the cookie dough balls. Bake for 9-11 minutes.

4 While the cookies cool, make the almond buttercream by beating the softened butter on high for 3-4 minutes until completely smooth. Add in the powdered sugar ½ cup at a time on low speed until fully mixed. Increase the speed to medium and add in the almond extract, vanilla extract, and 1 tbsp of heavy cream. If needed, add in 1-2 more tbsp of heavy cream to achieve the buttercream consistency you desire. Increase the speed to high and beat for 1 minute until fluffy and smooth. Transfer the buttercream to a piping bag fitted with a decorative tip. Frost the cooled sugar cookies and top with sprinkles.

BROWN SUGAR COOKIES

MAKES 10 COOKIES

Brown sugar cookies are a delightful twist on the classic sugar cookie that you didn't know you needed. With their soft, chewy texture and rich, caramel-like flavor, these cookies bring a deeper sweetness that sets them apart from traditional sugar cookies. The use of brown sugar adds a hint of molasses, giving each bite a warm, comforting taste that's simply irresistible. Perfect for any occasion, these cookies offer a familiar yet exciting flavor that will leave you wanting more—definitely a new favorite to add to your collection!

1 cup (120g) all-purpose flour, spooned and leveled

¼ teaspoon baking powder

¼ teaspoon baking soda

¼ teaspoon kosher salt

½ cup (113g) unsalted butter, softened

2/3 cup (145g) light brown sugar, packed

2 egg yolks, room temperature

1 teaspoon vanilla

1 Preheat the oven to 350°F (175°C) and line two baking sheets with parchment paper.

2 In a medium bowl, whisk together the all-purpose flour, baking powder, baking soda, and salt. Set this aside.

3 In a large mixing bowl, beat together the softened butter and brown sugar until light and fluffy, about two minutes. Add the egg yolks on medium speed one at a time until fully incorporated. Mix in the vanilla. Sprinkle in the dry ingredients and mix on low until just combined, be careful not to over-mix.

4 Using a 2-tablespoon size cookie scoop, scoop out the cookie dough and place on the prepared baking sheets. Bake six cookies at a time for 9 to 11 minutes until the edges are set and slightly more golden than the rest of the cookie. Allow the cookies to set on the baking sheet for 5 minutes before transferring to a wire cooling rack to finish cooling.

BROOKIE

MAKES 12 LARGE COOKIES

Can't choose between a chocolate cookie and chocolate chip? A Brookie is the best of both worlds! It's a soft chewy chocolate cookie, marbled with the most perfect chocolate chip cookie you've ever tasted. Rich cocoa and melty chocolate meets a buttery, chocolatey chip cookie is the ultimate cookie for any sweet treat lover.

FOR THE CHOCOLATE CHIP DOUGH

1⅓ cups (160g) all-purpose flour, spooned and leveled

½ teaspoon baking soda

½ teaspoon baking powder

½ teaspoon kosher salt

½ cup (113g) unsalted butter, softened

½ cup (105g) light brown sugar, packed

⅓ cup (70g) granulated sugar

1 large egg, room temperature

1 teaspoon vanilla extract

1 cup (170g) semisweet chocolate chips

FOR THE CHOCOLATE DOUGH

1⅓ cups (160g) all-purpose flour, spooned and leveled

⅓ cup (28g) Dutch processed cocoa powder

½ teaspoon baking soda

¼ teaspoon kosher salt

½ cup (113g) unsalted butter, softened

½ cup (105g) light brown sugar, packed

⅓ cup (67g) granulated sugar

1 large egg, room temperature

1 teaspoon vanilla extract

¾ cup (113g) semi-sweet chocolate chips, plus more for topping

1 Preheat the oven to 350°F (175°C) and line two baking sheets with parchment paper. Start by making the chocolate chip cookie dough. In a medium bowl, whisk together the all-purpose flour, baking soda, baking powder, and salt. Set this aside.

2 In a large mixing bowl, beat together the butter, brown sugar, and granulated sugar until light and fluffy, about 2 minutes. Add in the egg and vanilla, mixing on medium until incorporated. Scrape down the sides of the bowl. Sprinkle in the dry ingredients and mix on low until just combined. Using a rubber spatula, fold in the chocolate chips. Set the chocolate chip cookie dough aside while you make the chocolate dough.

3 In a medium mixing bowl, whisk together the all-purpose flour, cocoa powder, baking soda, and salt. Set this aside. In a large mixing bowl, beat together the butter, brown sugar, and granulated sugar until light and fluffy, about 2 minutes. Add in the egg and vanilla and mix until combined. Sprinkle in the dry ingredients and mix on low until just combined. Be careful not to overmix. Using a rubber spatula, fold in the semi-sweet chocolate chips.

4 Using a 2 tbsp sized cookie dough scoop, scoop out a ball of each dough. Roll each dough ball separately in your hands to form perfect balls and then press them together, rolling again to form a ball. Bake 6 cookies at a time for 9-12 minutes. Top the cookies with extra chocolate chips if desired.

CHAI CINNAMON ROLL SNICKERDOODLES

MAKES 12 COOKIES

A tradition I cannot wait to start with our future kids is homemade cinnamon rolls on Christmas morning. There's something so special about the dough rising all night, filling the house with that delicious smell of fresh baked pastries. Cinnamon rolls are a labor of love that turn out perfect every time. My secret ingredient? Adding chai spices. Trust me, this takes your cinnamon rolls to a whole new level and adds a delicious depth of flavor that is warm, sweet and unlike anything you've ever tasted. These chai cinnamon roll snickerdoodles are inspired by my famous chai cinnamon rolls and bring all the warm flavors of chai, to a chewy, buttery snickerdoodle.

FOR THE COOKIES

2¾ cups (330g) all-purpose flour, spooned and leveled

1 teaspoon baking soda

1 teaspoon baking powder

½ teaspoon kosher salt

2 teaspoons cinnamon

½ teaspoon nutmeg

¼ teaspoon ground cloves

1 cup (227g) unsalted butter, softened

¾ cup (160g) light brown sugar, packed

¾ cup (150g) granulated sugar

2 large eggs, room temperature

1 teaspoon vanilla extract

FOR THE FILLING

¼ cup (57g) unsalted butter, softened

½ cup (105g) light brown sugar

1 tablespoon granulated sugar

3 teaspoons cinnamon

½ teaspoon nutmeg

1 teaspoon vanilla extract

FOR THE ROLLING

1 cup (200g) granulated sugar

2 tablespoons cinnamon

½ teaspoon nutmeg

¼ teaspoon ground cloves

FOR THE ICING

1 cup powdered sugar

1 tablespoon milk

1 teaspoon vanilla bean paste or extract

½ teaspoon cinnamon

1. Preheat the oven to 350°F (175°C) and line two baking sheets with parchment paper. Make the cookies. In a medium bowl, whisk together the flour, baking soda, baking powder, salt, cinnamon, nutmeg, and ground cloves. Set this aside. In a large bowl, beat together the butter, brown sugar, and granulated sugar until light and fluffy, about 2 minutes. Add in the eggs one at a time until incorporated followed by the vanilla. Add in the dry ingredients and mix until just combined.

2. To make the cinnamon roll filling, beat together all the filling ingredients until combined. Scoop out a 3 tbsp sized ball of cookie dough, make a well in the center, and add in 1 tsp of cinnamon roll filling. Make sure to cover the filling completely and roll the dough in your hands to seal the edges.

3. In a small bowl, combine the rolling ingredients by whisking. Cover the dough ball in the rolling mixture and place on a parchment lined baking sheet. Bake for 9-11 minutes until the edges are firm. Make the icing while the cookies cool by mixing all the ingredients in a medium bowl. After the cookies are cool, drizzle the icing on top, and serve.

CHEWY CORN SUGAR COOKIES WITH HONEY BUTTERCREAM

MAKES 12 COOKIES

I have always been the biggest fan of a big, warm bowl of chili on a fall night paired with a buttery, sweet piece of cornbread. Really, chili is just an excuse to eat one of my favorite foods. The perfect cornbread is moist and tender on the inside, with a slightly crispy, golden crust. These cookies are the perfect slice of cornbread in cookie form! With their chewy, coarse texture from the cornmeal, they are then topped with a generous dollop of the sweetest, creamy honey buttercream. If you love cornbread as much as I do, you will love these cookies!

FOR THE COOKIES

1½ cups (180g) all-purpose flour, spooned and leveled

1 cup (120g) cornmeal

1 teaspoon baking soda

½ teaspoon baking powder

½ teaspoon kosher salt

1 cup (227g) unsalted butter, softened

1 cup (200g) granulated sugar

½ cup (105g) light brown sugar, packed

1 large egg, room temperature

1 egg yolk, room temperature

1½ teaspoons vanilla extract

FOR THE BUTTERCREAM

1 cup (227g) unsalted butter, softened

2 cups (240g) powdered sugar

1-3 tablespoons heavy cream

1 tablespoon honey

1 teaspoon vanilla extract

⅛ teaspoon kosher salt

1 In a bowl, whisk together the all-purpose flour, cornmeal, baking soda, baking powder, and salt. Set this aside. In a large mixing bowl, beat together the softened butter, granulated sugar, and light brown sugar until the mixture is light and fluffy, about 2 minutes. Beat in the egg and egg yolk one at a time, mixing well after each addition. Add the vanilla extract and mix until fully incorporated. Gradually add the dry ingredients to the wet ingredients, mixing on low speed until just combined. Be careful not to overmix the dough. Chill the dough in the refrigerator for at least 30 minutes. This step helps the cookies maintain their shape and enhance the chewiness.

2 During the last 15 minutes of chill time, preheat the oven to 350°F (175°C) and line two baking sheets with parchment paper. Using a 2 tbsp cookie scoop, scoop out cookie dough balls and place them on the prepared baking sheets. Bake for 8-10 minutes, or until the edges are lightly golden but the centers are still soft and pale.

3 While the cookies cool, make the honey buttercream. In a mixing bowl, beat the softened butter on high until light and creamy, about 3 minutes. Slowly add in the powdered sugar on low speed and mix until combine. Add 1 tbsp cream, honey, vanilla extract, and salt and beat until combined. Add an additional 1-2 more tbsp of heavy cream if a thinner consistency is desired. Transfer the butter cream to a piping bag and frost the cooled, corn cookies.

EVERYTHING KITCHEN SINK COOKIES

MAKES 12 COOKIES

These cookies were inspired by my dad, who could eat potato chips for dinner. Salty and sweet is the best flavor combo in the world, and these cookies really have it all. They are packed full of gooey, melty white chocolate, semi-sweet and peanut butter chips, salty potato chips, and crunchy pretzels. They are the best of all worlds!

1⅓ cups (160g) all-purpose flour, spooned and leveled

½ teaspoon baking soda

½ teaspoon baking powder

½ teaspoon kosher salt

½ cup (113g) unsalted butter, softened

⅓ cup (70g) granulated sugar

½ cup (105g) light brown sugar, packed

1 large egg, room temperature

1 teaspoon vanilla extract

½ cup (85g) semi-sweet chocolate chips, plus more for topping

¼ cup (43g) white chocolate chips, plus more for topping

¼ cup (43g) peanut butter chips, plus more for topping

¼ cup (30g) mini pretzels, roughly chopped, plus more for topping

¼ cup (15g) potato chips, roughly chopped, plus more for topping

1. Preheat the oven to 350°F (175°C) and line two baking sheets with parchment paper.

2. In a medium bowl, whisk together the flour, baking soda, baking powder, and salt. Set this aside.

3. In a large bowl, beat together the butter, granulated sugar, and brown sugar on high until light and fluffy, about 2 minutes. Scrape down the sides of the bowl. Reduce the speed to low and add the egg and vanilla and mix until combined. Sprinkle in the dry ingredients and mix until just combined, but steaks remain. Using a rubber spatula, fold in the semi-sweet chocolate chips, white chocolate chips, peanut butter chips, chopped mini pretzels, and chopped potato chips into the dough.

4. Using a 3 tbsp sized cookie dough scoop, scoop out 12 cookie dough balls and place them on the prepared baking sheets with 2 inches in between each ball. Bake for 9-11 minutes until the edges just start to turn slightly golden. Top with additional mix ins if desired, this will make the cookies even more beautiful. Allow the cookies to cool on the pan for 5 minutes before transferring to a wire rack to continue cooling.

PEANUT BUTTER CUP COOKIES

MAKES 10 COOKIES

Name a better pairing than peanut butter and chocolate? It's a favorite for a reason! These peanut butter cup cookies start with a chewy, peanut butter cookie topped with a smooth, rich layer of chocolate fudge ganache and then topped with the good stuff: loads of chopped peanut butter cups! If you are a chocolate peanut butter lover, these will be your favorite cookie!

FOR THE COOKIES

1 cup (120g) all-purpose flour, spooned and leveled

½ teaspoon baking soda

½ teaspoon baking powder

¼ teaspoon kosher salt

½ cup (113g) unsalted butter, softened

¾ cup (160g) light brown sugar, packed

¼ cup (50g) granulated sugar

1 large egg, room temperature

1 egg yolk, room temperature

1½ teaspoons vanilla extract

⅓ cup creamy peanut butter, like Jif (plus a little more for topping)

1 tablespoon honey

3 peanut butter cups, roughly chopped for topping

FOR THE GANACHE

½ cup (85g) milk chocolate chips

1 tablespoon heavy cream

1 Preheat the oven to 350°F (175°C) and line two baking sheets with parchment paper.

2 In a medium bowl, whisk together the flour, baking soda, baking powder, and salt and set aside. In a large bowl, beat the butter, brown sugar, and granulated sugar for 2 minutes until creamy and light. Add in the egg, egg yolk, and vanilla and mix for an additional 2 minutes until fluffy. Add in the peanut butter and honey and mix until combined. Sprinkle in the dry ingredients and mix until just combined.

3 Scoop out 3 tbsp sized dough balls and place on the parchment lined baking sheets 2 inches apart to allow for spreading. Bake for 8-10 minutes, until the edges are just slightly darker than the center of the cookie.

4 While the cookies cool, make the chocolate fudge ganache. Add the chocolate chips and heavy cream to a microwave safe bowl, and microwave for 45 seconds. Allow the ganache to sit for 1 minute before vigorously whisking until smooth and glossy.

5 Top the cooled peanut butter cookies with a generous layer of chocolate fudge ganache, a swirl of extra peanut butter, and chopped peanut butter cups.

CHOCOLATE MOLTEN LAVA COOKIES

MAKES 10 COOKIES

The best surprise is biting into a cookie and finding out there is molten, chocolate fudge inside. YUM! These chocolate molten lava cookie are chewy, fudgy chocolate cookies with the most decadent, melty fudge inside. They are perfect for a Valentine's Day dessert table or just because you need something extra chocolatey any night of the week!

FOR THE COOKIES

1½ cups (188g) all-purpose flour, spooned and leveled

½ cup (40g) Dutch processed cocoa powder

½ teaspoon baking powder

½ teaspoon kosher salt

¾ cup (170g) unsalted butter, softened

¾ cup (160g) light brown sugar, packed

¼ cup (50g) granulated white sugar

2 egg yolks, room temperature

1½ teaspoons vanilla extract

Powdered sugar, for dusting on top

FOR THE FUDGE FILLING

¼ cup hot fudge, cold

1. Preheat the oven to 350°F (175°C) and line two baking sheets with parchment paper.

2. In a medium bowl, whisk together the flour, cocoa powder, baking powder, and salt. Set this aside.

3. In a large mixing bowl, beat together the butter, brown sugar, and granulated sugar until light and fluffy, about 2 minutes. Reduce the speed to medium low and add in the egg yolks one at a time until fully incorporated. Mix in the vanilla.

4. Gradually add in the dry ingredients and mix on low until just combined. Scoop out 3-tablespoon sized balls of dough, create a well in the center, and add 1 teaspoon cold hot fudge. Close the dough completely around the hot fudge, and roll the dough balls in your hands to form perfect circles and close the seams.

5. Place the cookie dough balls on the prepared baking sheets and bake for 9-11 minutes. Allow the cookies to cool, dust powdered sugar over the tops, and enjoy!

BAKERY STYLE PEANUT BUTTER COOKIES

MAKES 8 LARGE COOKIES

When I travel to New York, the one thing my husband asks me to bring back for him is one thick, chewy peanut butter chocolate cookie. Now that I'm sharing my secret recipe with you, there's no need to hop on a plane to fetch your bakery style cookies! This thick, chewy cookie is perfectly soft and doughy on the inside with a slightly crispy exterior. It's packed full of peanut butter candy, melty peanut butter, and chocolate chips. Have a glass of cold milk handy to perfectly compliment the richness of this heavenly, warm cookie!

2½ cups (300g) cake flour, sifted

1½ teaspoons baking powder

1 teaspoon baking soda

¾ teaspoon kosher salt

½ cup (113g) unsalted butter, softened

1 cup (210g) light brown sugar, packed

¼ cup (50g) granulated sugar

2 large eggs, room temperature

1 teaspoon vanilla extract

1 cup (170g) Reese's pieces

1 cup (170g) peanut butter chips

1 cup (170g) semi-sweet chocolate chips

1   In a medium bowl, whisk together the sifted cake flour, baking powder, baking soda, and salt. Set this aside.

2   In a large mixing bowl, beat together the butter, brown sugar, and granulated white sugar until smooth and creamy, about 2 minutes. Add in one egg at a time, mixing on medium low until fully incorporated. Add in the vanilla and mix until combined. Sprinkle in the dry ingredients and mix until just combined. Fold in the Reese's Pieces, peanut butter chips, and semi-sweet chocolate chips with a rubber spatula. Scoop out 5oz of cookie dough and roughly roll them into balls. The dough will be slightly sticky so wash your hands in between rolling each cookie dough ball. Place all 8 cookie dough balls on a parchment paper lined baking sheet, and transfer to the refrigerator to chill for 1 hour.

3   During the last 15 minutes of chill time, preheat the oven to 375°F (190°C) and line a second baking sheet with parchment paper. Place 4 cookie dough balls on each baking sheet (you can re-roll them slightly if needed as the dough will be easier to work with). Bake for 11-15 minutes. Start watching the cookies at the 10-minute mark. They are done when the tops become golden brown. Allow the cookies to set on the baking sheet for at least 20 minutes before transferring to a wire cooling rack.

SALTED DARK CHOCOLATE PISTACHIO TOFFEE COOKIES

MAKE 12 COOKIES

These indulgent salted dark chocolate pistachio toffee cookies combine rich, velvety dark chocolate with crunchy pistachios and buttery toffee bits for an irresistible mix of flavor and texture. Each decadent bite is the perfect balance of sweet and salty. The toffee melts into little pools of chewy caramel, and paired with the crunchy pistachios, these cookies are packed with layers of rich, bold flavors. If you love salty and sweet, these cookies were made for you.

1⅓ cups (160g) all-purpose flour, spooned and leveled

½ teaspoon baking soda

½ teaspoon baking powder

½ teaspoon kosher salt

½ cup (113g) salted butter, softened

⅓ cup (70g) granulated sugar

½ cup (105g) light brown sugar, packed

1 large egg, room temperature

1 teaspoon vanilla extract

½ cup (85g) dark chocolate chunks, plus more for topping

½ cup (75g) pistachios, chopped

½ cup (85g) toffee bits

Flaky sea salt, for topping

1. Preheat the oven to 350°F (175°C) and line two baking sheets with parchment paper.

2. In a medium bowl, whisk together the flour, baking soda, baking powder, and salt. Set this aside.

3. In a large bowl, beat together the butter, granulated sugar, and brown sugar on high until light and fluffy, about 2 minutes. Scrape down the sides of the bowl. Reduce the speed to low and add the egg and vanilla and mix until combined. Sprinkle in the dry ingredients and mix until just combined, but steaks remain. Using a rubber spatula, fold the dark chocolate chunks, chopped pistachios, and toffee bits into the dough.

4. Using a 3-tablespoon sized cookie dough scoop, scoop out 12 cookie dough balls and place them on the prepared baking sheets with 2 inches in between each ball. Bake for 9-11 minutes until the edges just start to turn slightly golden. Top with additional chocolate chunks and flaky sea salt. Allow the cookies to cool on the pan for 5 minutes before transferring to a wire rack to continue cooling.

FRUITY

CHOCOLATE ORANGE COOKIES

MAKES 12 COOKIES

Everyone I make these orange chocolate cookies for falls in LOVE with them! I include them every year in my holiday cookie boxes, and my friends and family talk about them all year long counting down the days until their holiday cookie box is delivered on their doorstep. Now, you too can experience just how spectacular these cookies are as I share my secret recipe with you. Made with a whole entire milk chocolate orange, these cookies are packed full of creamy, citrusy chocolate in every bite. Orange chocolate has always been one of my favorite flavor combinations making these the perfect cookie!

1¼ cups (160g) all-purpose flour, spooned and leveled

½ teaspoon baking soda

½ teaspoon kosher salt

½ cup (113g) unsalted butter, softened

½ cup (105g) light brown sugar, packed

¼ cup (50g) granulated sugar

1 large egg, room temperature

½ teaspoon vanilla extract

½ teaspoon orange extract

1 cup (170g) semi-sweet chocolate chips

½ Terry's milk chocolate orange, roughly chopped (save the other half for topping)

1. Preheat the oven to 350°F (175°C) and line two baking sheets with parchment paper.

2. In a medium bowl, whisk together the all-purpose flour, baking soda, and salt. Set this aside.

3. In a large mixing bowl, beat the softened butter, brown sugar, and granulated sugar until light and fluffy, about 2 minutes. Add in the egg, vanilla, and orange extract and mix on medium until combined. Sprinkle in the dry ingredients and mix on low until just combined. Using a rubber spatula, gently fold in the chocolate chips and chopped Terry's orange chocolate.

4. Scoop out 3 tbsp size balls of dough onto your cookie sheet and bake for 10-12 minutes. Once out of the oven, add extra Terry's chocolate orange slices on top. Allow to cool on a wire rack and serve.

CHOCOLATE CHIP BANANA BREAD COOKIES WITH CREAM CHEESE FROSTING

MAKES 12 COOKIES

Growing up, my mom would make the best chocolate chip banana bread in the world almost every week. Every Sunday, our house would smell like fresh baked banana bread, and we would cut slices off the delicious loaf all week long to pack in our lunches or to snack on after school. One of my favorite ways to eat chocolate chip banana bread is with a thick layer of cream cheese on top. Trust me, it is the most delicious thing ever! These chocolate chip banana bread cookies were inspired by the loaves my mom would always make. These cookies have a unique, soft cake-like texture to them, and taste just like you're taking a bite out of a warm slice of banana bread.

FOR THE COOKIES

2 cups (240g) all-purpose flour, spooned and leveled

1 teaspoon baking soda

½ teaspoon kosher salt

½ cup (113g) unsalted butter, softened

1 cup (200g) granulated sugar

1 large egg, room temperature

1½ teaspoons vanilla extract

1 cup (250g) mashed ripe banana, about 2 large bananas

1 cup (170g) semi-sweet chocolate chips

FOR THE FROSTING

3 ounces (84g) cream cheese, softened

2 tablespoons (28g) unsalted butter, softened

¾ cup (190g) powdered sugar

1 teaspoon vanilla extract

1-2 tablespoons heavy cream or milk

1   Preheat the oven to 350°F (175°C) and line two baking sheets with parchment paper. In a medium bowl, whisk together the flour, baking soda, and salt and set aside.

2   In a large mixing bowl, beat the butter and sugar on high until light and fluffy, about 2 minutes. Add in the egg and vanilla and mix until combined. Add in the mashed banana and mix until incorporated. Sprinkle in the dry ingredients and mix until just combined. Fold in the chocolate chips.

3   Using a 3-tablespoon sized cookie dough scoop, drop dollops of cookie dough batter 2 inches apart on the prepared baking sheets. The dough will be almost like banana bread batter, but slightly thicker. Bake for 9-11 minutes until the edges start to turn golden brown.

4   While the cookies cool, make the cream cheese icing by beating together the cream cheese and butter on high. Add in the powdered sugar and beat on low, slowly increasing the speed to high for 2 minutes. Add in the vanilla and 1 tbsp heavy cream and mix until combined. To reach your desired consistency, add in an additional 1 tbsp of heavy cream if needed. Spoon the icing over the tops of the completely cooled cookies. Top with nuts or additional chocolate chips if desired.

CHERRY PIE SHORTBREAD SUGAR COOKIES

MAKES 10 COOKIES

Every summer for the 4th of July, I make a buttery, sweet cherry pie for our BBQ! These cookies are loaded full of juicy cherries and topped with sweet, vanilla icing. What's better than a whole cherry pie? Individual cherry pie shortbread cookies! They are the perfect individual sized desserts to bring to your next cookout for everyone to share!

FOR THE COOKIES

2½ cups (300g) all-purpose flour, spooned and leveled

½ teaspoon baking powder

½ teaspoon kosher salt

1 cup (227g) unsalted butter, softened

1 cup (200g) granulated sugar

1 large egg yolk, room temperature

1 teaspoon vanilla extract

½ teaspoon almond extract

FOR THE CHERRY FILLING

2 cups sweet cherries, pitted

¼ cup water

1 teaspoon lemon juice

¼ cup (50g) sugar

1 tablespoon cornstarch

¼ teaspoon vanilla extract

FOR THE ICING

½ cup (60g) powdered sugar

1-2 tablespoons milk

¼ teaspoon vanilla extract

1. Preheat the oven to 350°F (175°C) and line two baking sheets with parchment paper. In a medium bowl, whisk together the flour, baking powder, and salt. Set this aside. In a large bowl, beat together the butter and granulated sugar on high until light and fluffy, about 2 minutes. Add the egg yolk, vanilla, and almond extract and mix on medium speed until incorporated. Sprinkle in the dry ingredients and mix on low until just combined.

2. Using a 3-tablespoon sized cookie dough scoop, scoop out cookie dough balls, roll them in your hands, and place them on the prepared baking sheets. Press them down with your hand to flatten them slightly. Bake for 9-11 minutes until the edges start to turn just slightly golden. Immediately out of the oven, gently press down the centers of the cookies with a tablespoon to create a little well in the center for the cherry pie filling.

3. While the cookies cool, make the cherry pie filling by adding the pitted cherries, water, lemon juice, sugar, and cornstarch to a medium saucepan. Mix the ingredients well and bring the mixture to a boil. Reduce the heat to low and let the cherry filling simmer for 10 minutes while stirring frequently. Take the cherry filling off the heat, mix in the vanilla, and allow it to fully cool.

4. Make the vanilla icing by adding the powdered sugar, milk, and vanilla to a bowl. Whisk to combine until smooth and creamy. If the icing is too thick, add an additional ½ -2 tsp of milk. Assemble the cookies by adding a dollop of cherry pie filling to the center of the cookie. Drizzle the vanilla icing on top.

FROSTED LEMON CURD POPPYSEED CAKE COOKIES

MAKES 12 COOKIES

My favorite springtime dessert is anything lemon curd poppyseed flavor! These chewy, sweet lemon poppyseed sugar cookies are topped with zesty lemon buttercream and lusciously smooth lemon curd. If you're in need of a springtime dessert, this is it! These lemon cookies will be the most beautiful addition to your Easter table.

FOR THE COOKIES

2 cups (240g) all-purpose flour, spooned and leveled

½ teaspoon baking soda

½ teaspoon baking powder

1 teaspoon cornstarch

½ teaspoon kosher salt

2 tablespoons poppy seeds

¾ cup (150g) granulated sugar

¼ cup (53g) light brown sugar, packed

1 tablespoon lemon zest, about 1 large lemon

½ cup (113 g) unsalted butter, softened

1 large egg, room temperature

1 teaspoon vanilla

2 teaspoons lemon juice

½ cup lemon curd, for topping

FOR THE FROSTING

4 tablespoons (56g) unsalted butter, softened

4 ounces (112g) cream cheese, softened

2½ cups (300g) powdered sugar

½ teaspoon vanilla extract

2 tablespoons lemon juice

1 tablespoon lemon zest

¼ teaspoon kosher salt

1   Preheat the oven to 350°F (175°C) and line two baking sheets with parchment paper. In a medium bowl, whisk together all-purpose flour, baking soda, baking powder, cornstarch, salt, and poppy seeds. Set this aside.

2   In a large mixing bowl add the granulated sugar, brown sugar, and lemon zest. Rub the lemon zest into the sugars with your fingers to release the oils from the lemons. Add the butter to the mixing bowl with the lemon zest and sugars, and beat on high until light and fluffy, about two minutes. Add in the egg, vanilla, and lemon juice, mixing on medium until well combined. Sprinkle in the dry ingredients and mix on low until just combined. Scoop out 3 tablespoons size cookie dough balls, roll in your hands, and place on the prepared baking sheets. Bake six cookies at a time for 9-11 minutes until the edges just start to set.

3   While the cookies cool, make the lemon cream cheese frosting. Using a mixer, beat the butter and cream cheese on high until smooth. Add the powdered sugar ½ cup at a time and mix until smooth. Mix in the vanilla, lemon juice, lemon zest, and salt and beat on high for 1 minute until fluffy and smooth. Transfer the frosting to a piping bag fitted with a decorative tip. Assemble the cookies by piping the frosting over the whole cookie. Make a higher rim of frosting around the border of the cookie. Fill the center of the cookie with 2 teaspoons of lemon curd. Sprinkle on some additional poppyseeds.

BLUEBERRY MUFFIN COOKIES

MAKES 12 COOKIES

Growing up in Colorado during the winter was like living in a snow globe. When the snow would fall, the world would turn peaceful and the only sound would be the snowflakes falling on the pine trees outside. I had a tradition that every time it would snow, I would bake a big batch of warm blueberry muffins. These blueberry muffin cookies are loaded with plump, juicy blueberries and topped with a sugary, buttery streusel. They taste just like the muffins I make each winter, in cookie form and I hope you enjoy them the next time the snow starts to fall.

FOR THE STREUSEL

¼ cup (50g) granulated sugar

¼ cup (53g) light brown sugar, packed

½ cup (60g) all-purpose flour, spooned and leveled

½ teaspoon cinnamon

4 tablespoons (57g) unsalted butter, softened

FOR THE COOKIES

2½ cups (300g) all-purpose flour, spooned and leveled

½ teaspoon baking powder

½ teaspoon baking soda

¼ teaspoon kosher salt

1 cup (227g) unsalted butter, room temperature

1⅓ cups (267g) granulated sugar

1 large egg, room temperature

1½ teaspoons vanilla extract

1 cup fresh blueberries

1. Make the streusel by adding the granulated sugar, brown sugar, all-purpose flour, and cinnamon to a small bowl. Stir in the softened butter, then use your hands to mix all the ingredients until a crumb like texture forms. Set this aside.

2. Preheat the oven to 350°F (175°C) and line two baking sheets with parchment paper. Make the cookies. In a medium bowl, whisk together the flour, baking powder, baking soda, and salt. Set this aside. In a large mixing bowl, beat together the softened butter and granulated sugar on high until it's light and fluffy. About 2 minutes. Add the egg and vanilla extract and mix until combined. Sprinkle in the dry ingredients and mix on low until just combined. Use a rubber spatula to carefully fold in the blueberries, making sure they do not smash into the dough. If you use frozen blueberries, it will add more moisture to the dough making the cookies spread more while baking and be thinner. It will also transfer more blueberry juice to the dough making your cookies bluer in color. Add an additional 2 tbsp all-purpose flour if using frozen blueberries, though I do recommend fresh.

3. Using a 3-tablespoon sized cookie scoop, scoop out cookie dough, balls, roll them in your hands, and place them on the prepared baking sheets. Add the streusel crumb to the tops and the sides of each cookie dough ball and bake for 9-11 minutes.

PIÑA COLADA SUGAR COOKIE

MAKES 12 COOKIES

These pina colada sugar cookies will transport you to being sun kissed on a soft sandy beach with a creamy and smooth frozen beverage in your hand. With a luscious coconut sugar cookie base, these cookies are then topped with the sweetest, fruity pineapple buttercream. You don't even need PTO to enjoy a vacation with these cookies!

FOR THE COOKIES

2¾ cups (330g) all-purpose flour, spooned and leveled

1 teaspoon baking soda

½ teaspoon baking powder

½ teaspoon kosher salt

1 cup (227g) unsalted butter, softened

1 cup (200g) granulated sugar

½ cup (105g) light brown sugar, packed

1 large egg, room temperature

1 egg yolk, room temperature

1½ teaspoons coconut extract

1 teaspoon vanilla extract

½ cup (55g) dried coconut

Pineapple slices for topping, if desired

FOR THE BUTTERCREAM

1 cup (113g) unsalted butter, softened

3 cups (360g) powdered sugar

½ teaspoon coconut extract

2 tablespoons pineapple juice

¼ teaspoon kosher salt

1 In a medium bowl, whisk together the flour, baking soda, baking powder, and salt. Set this aside. In a large mixing bowl beat together on high the butter, granulated sugar, and brown sugar until light and fluffy, about two minutes. Add the egg, egg yolk, coconut extract, and vanilla extract. Mix on medium until combined. Sprinkle in the dry ingredients and mix on low until just combined. Fold the coconut into the dough with a rubber spatula.

2 Cover the dough tightly, and chill for 30 minutes in the refrigerator. During the last 15 minutes of chill time, preheat the oven to 350°F (175°C) and line two baking sheets with parchment paper. Using a three-tablespoon sized cookie scoop, scoop out the cookie dough and place on the prepared baking sheets. Bake 6 cookies at a time for 10-12 minutes. Allow the cookies to set on the baking sheet for 5 minutes before transferring to a wire cooling rack to cool completely.

3 While the cookies cool, make the pineapple coconut buttercream. Beat the softened butter on high for 3 minutes until completely smooth and creamy. Add in the powdered sugar ½ cup at a time, mixing on low until combined. Add in the coconut extract, pineapple juice, and salt. Increase the speed slowly until a high speed is reached. Beat together all the ingredients for an additional 1 minute until the buttercream is light and smooth. Transfer the frosting to a piping bag fitted with a decorative tip. Assemble the cookies by piping the frosting onto the cooled coconut sugar cookies. Top with a pineapple slice if desired.

WHITE CHOCOLATE ALMOND RASPBERRY COOKIES

MAKES 12 COOKIES

My favorite flavor combination of all time is white chocolate almond raspberry. Cakes, cookies, cupcakes, give me ALL the white chocolate almond raspberry treats! These chewy almond cookies are studded with melty white chocolate chips and juicy raspberries. They are creamy, indulgent and are perfect year-round!

1½ cups (190g) all-purpose flour, spooned and leveled

½ teaspoon baking soda

¼ teaspoon kosher salt

½ cup (113g) unsalted butter, softened

½ cup (100g) granulated sugar

½ cup (105g) light brown sugar, packed

1 large egg, room temperature

1 teaspoon vanilla extract

½ teaspoon almond extract

¾ cup (135g) white chocolate chips

½ cup fresh raspberries, frozen for 15 minutes before use

1   Preheat your oven to 350°F (175°C) and line two baking sheets with parchment paper.

2   In a medium bowl, whisk together the all-purpose flour, baking soda, and salt. Set this aside.

3   In a large bowl, beat the softened butter, granulated sugar, and brown sugar together until smooth and creamy, about 2-3 minutes. Mix in the egg, vanilla extract, and almond extract until fully combined. Slowly add the dry ingredients to the wet mixture, stirring until just combined. Do not overmix.

4   Using a rubber spatula, very gently fold in the white chocolate chips and the slightly frozen raspberries. Freezing the raspberries helps prevent them from breaking apart too much in the dough. Take care not to smash the raspberries too much as this will add moisture to the dough making your cookies soggy and could turn them a blueish hue as they bake.

5   Scoop 3 tbsp cookie dough balls onto the prepared baking sheets. Bake for 10-12 minutes or until the edges are lightly golden, and the centers are set. Allow the cookies to cool on the baking sheet for 5 minutes before transferring to a wire rack to cool completely.

BLACKBERRY CHEESECAKE COOKIES

MAKES 10 COOKIES

Making a whole entire cheesecake can be a daunting task and requires lots of kitchen gadgets and equipment. These blackberry cheesecake cookies are packed full of all the delicious flavors and textures of cheesecake, without all the hassle. It all starts with a chewy, graham cracker sugar cookie, topped with cream cheese frosting, and juicy sweet blackberry filling. These blackberry cheesecake cookies are the perfect, individual sized dessert to share with all your family and friends!

FOR THE COOKIES

1 2/3 cups (200g) all-purpose flour, spooned and leveled

½ teaspoon baking powder

½ teaspoon baking soda

½ teaspoon kosher salt

¼ cup (15g) graham cracker crumbs, about 1 sheet, plus more for topping

½ cup (113g) unsalted butter, softened

¾ cup (150g) granulated sugar

¼ cup (53g) light brown sugar, packed

1 large egg, room temperature

1 teaspoon vanilla extract

FOR THE FROSTING

4 ounces (112g) cream cheese, softened

4 tablespoons (56g) unsalted butter, softened

2½ cups (300g) powdered sugar

½ teaspoon vanilla extract

¼ teaspoon kosher salt

¼ cup blackberry jam, for topping

10 fresh blackberries, for topping

1   Preheat the oven to 350°F (175°C) and line two baking sheets with parchment paper.

2   In a medium bowl, whisk together the all-purpose flour, baking powder, baking soda, salt, and graham cracker crumbs (you can smash these with your hands or a food processor). Set this aside.

3   Using a stand mixer, beat together the butter, granulated sugar, and brown sugar until smooth. Add in the egg and vanilla extract and mix on medium low until incorporated. Sprinkle in the dry ingredients and mix on low until just combined.

4   Scoop 3 tbsp sized balls of cookie dough, roll into perfect balls, and place onto the prepared cookie sheets. Bake for 9-11 minutes until the edges are slightly golden brown.

5   While the cookies cool, make the cream cheese frosting. Beat together the cream cheese and butter until light and fluffy (about 3-4 minutes). Slowly add in the powdered sugar ½ cup at a time and mix on low until all combined. Add in the vanilla extract and salt and beat on high for 1 minute until fluffy and smooth. Scoop the cream cheese frosting into a piping bag and frost the cookies. Add a 1 tsp sized dollop of blackberry jam to the center of the cookie and top with a fresh blackberry.

COOKIE BUTTER WHITE CHOCOLATE BANANA PUDDING COOKIES

MAKES 12 COOKIES

One of my favorite things to do in NYC is to enjoy all the incredible food! Banana pudding is a classic New York treat, and these cookie butter white chocolate banana pudding cookies are the perfect dessert to bake up when you cannot make it out to the city. They are the perfect balance of creamy cookie butter, velvety white chocolate chips, and ripe banana all topped with a vanilla pudding frosting. Since there are bananas in these, you have my full permission to eat them for breakfast!

FOR THE COOKIES

2¾ cups (330g) all-purpose flour, spooned and leveled

1 teaspoon baking soda

1 teaspoon kosher salt

¾ cup Biscoff cookie crumbs

1 cup (230g, about 2 large bananas) ripe bananas, mashed

1 cup (227g) unsalted butter, softened

1 cup (200g) granulated sugar

½ cup (105g) light brown sugar, packed

1 large egg yolk, room temperature

1 teaspoon vanilla extract

½ cup (85g) white chocolate chips

FOR THE FROSTING

1 cup (236ml) heavy cream, cold

¼ cup (30g) powdered sugar

½ teaspoon vanilla extract

2 ounces instant vanilla pudding mix

¼ cup Biscoff cookie crumbs, for topping

1. Preheat the oven to 350°F (175°C) and line two baking sheets with parchment paper. In a medium bowl whisk together the flour, baking soda, and salt. Set this aside. In a food processor, add the Biscoff cookies and pulse until a fine crumb forms. Measure out ¾ cup of the crumbs for the cookie dough. Pulse an additional ¼ cup and set aside for topping the cookies. On a plate, mash the two bananas.

2. In a large bowl, beat together the softened butter, granulated sugar, and brown sugar on high until light and creamy, about two minutes. Add in the egg yolk, vanilla, and mashed bananas. Mix on medium until well combined. Sprinkle in the dry ingredients and mix on low until just combined. Add in the Biscoff cookie crumbs and white chocolate chips and fold in with a rubber spatula. Scoop out 3 tbsp sized cookie dough balls and place 6 at a time on the prepared parchment lined baking sheets. Bake for 9-11 minutes until the edges are slightly golden.

3. While the cookies cool, prepare the vanilla pudding frosting. In a large bowl, add the heavy cream, powdered sugar, and vanilla extract. Beat until soft peaks form. Sprinkle in the vanilla pudding mix and beat together until thick and creamy. If the frosting appears separated, add an additional tbsp of heavy cream as needed until the frosting is smooth. Spread a layer of vanilla pudding frosting on each cookie, top with Biscoff cookie crumbs, a Biscoff cookie, and sliced bananas if desired.

ALMOST TOO PRETTY TO EAT

TIRAMISU COOKIES

MAKES 10 COOKIES

This tiramisu cookie is a luscious combination of espresso, mascarpone, and cocoa, delivering the rich flavors of the classic dessert in a chewy, irresistible bite. With notes of bold coffee, creamy mascarpone, and a light dusting of cocoa powder, this cookie captures the essence of tiramisu in a perfectly balanced, indulgent treat. It's the ultimate cookie for those who crave a sophisticated yet comforting dessert.

FOR THE COOKIES

2 cups (230g) all-purpose flour, spooned and leveled

½ teaspoon baking powder

½ teaspoon baking soda

1 tablespoon ground espresso powder

½ teaspoon kosher salt

½ cup (113g) unsalted butter, softened

½ cup (100g) granulated sugar

½ cup (106g) light brown sugar, packed

1 large egg, room temperature

1 teaspoon vanilla extract

FOR THE MASCARPONE CREAM

5 ounces mascarpone, room temperature

1 cup (113g) powdered sugar

1 teaspoon vanilla extract

1 cup (240g) heavy cream, room temperature

1 teaspoon espresso powder

Cocoa powder, for dusting

1   Preheat the oven to 350°F (175°C) and line two baking sheets with parchment paper. In a medium bowl, whisk together the flour, baking powder, baking soda, espresso powder, and salt. Set this aside.

2   In a large mixing bowl, beat together the butter, granulated sugar, and brown sugar on high until light and fluffy, about 2 minutes. Reduce the speed to medium low and add in the egg and vanilla until well incorporated. On low, gradually add in the dry ingredients, mixing until just combined.

3   Using a 3 tbsp sized cookie scoop, scoop out the dough, roll it in your hands to form a perfect circle, and place it on the prepared baking sheets. Bake one tray at a time for 9-11 minutes. Allow the cookies to fully cool while you make the mascarpone cream.

4   To make the mascarpone cream, add all the ingredients to a mixing bowl and beat on high for 2-3 minutes until stiff peaks form. Transfer the mascarpone cream to a piping bag fitted with a decorative tip. Frost the cooled cookies, dust with cocoa powder, and serve!

PEANUT BUTTER AND JELLY COOKIES

MAKES 12 COOKIES

There's no more classic combination than peanut butter and jelly! With a chewy, nutty peanut butter cookie base, these cookies are then frosted with the most delicious creamy peanut butter buttercream and your favorite jam. They are perfectly chewy with a soft, gooey center, just like a nostalgic PB&J. These peanut butter and jelly cookies are just as delicious as they are beautiful!

FOR THE COOKIE

1 cup (120g) all-purpose flour, spooned and leveled

½ teaspoon baking soda

½ teaspoon baking powder

¼ teaspoon kosher salt

½ cup (113g) unsalted butter, softened

¾ cup (160g) light brown sugar, packed

¼ cup (50g) granulated sugar

1 large egg, room temperature

1½ teaspoons vanilla extract

⅓ cup (90g) creamy peanut butter, I prefer Jif

FOR THE FROSTING SWIRL

½ cup (113g) unsalted butter, softened

¼ teaspoon kosher salt

4 cups (450g) powdered sugar

½ cup (135g) creamy peanut butter, full sugar, not natural

2 teaspoons vanilla extract

3 tablespoons heavy cream

FOR THE JELLY SWIRL

½ cup jelly (Flavor of your choice)

1. Preheat the oven to 350°F (175°C) and line two baking sheets with parchment paper. In a medium bowl, whisk together the flour, baking soda, baking powder, and salt and set aside.

2. In a large bowl, cream together the butter, brown sugar, and granulated sugar for 2 minutes until creamy and light. Add in the egg and vanilla and mix for an additional 2 minutes until fluffy. Add in the peanut butter and mix until combined. Sprinkle in the dry ingredients and mix until just combined, there will be some streaks. Scoop out 3 tbsp sized dough balls and place on the parchment lined baking sheets 2 inches apart to allow for spreading. Bake for 8-10 minutes, until the edges are just slightly darker than the center of the cookie. Allow the cookies to cool on the baking sheet for a few minutes before transferring to a wire rack to continue cooling.

3. While the cookies cool, make the peanut butter buttercream by beating together the butter and salt until light and fluffy, about 3 minutes. Scrape down the sides of the bowl. Add in the powdered sugar, peanut butter, vanilla extract, and heavy cream. Beat on low and then slowly increase the speed to high and beat until the frosting is smooth and creamy. Transfer the peanut butter buttercream to a piping bag. Add the jelly to a piping bag. Swirl the peanut butter buttercream onto each completely cool cookie. Swirl the jelly inside the peanut butter swirl.

RED VELVET TOASTED S'MORES COOKIES

MAKES 10 COOKIES

Red velvet and s'mores combined? An unexpected match made in heaven! These chocolatey, cocoa filled chewy red velvet cookies are topped with melty chocolate fudge ganache and then topped with a generous dollop of marshmallow meringue frosting. The toasted marshmallow pairs perfectly with all the chocolate in this cookie. These red velvet smores cookies are best enjoyed around the bonfire year round!

FOR THE COOKIES

½ cup (113g) unsalted butter, browned

1 2/3 cups (200g) all-purpose flour, spooned and leveled

½ teaspoon baking powder

½ teaspoon baking soda

1 tablespoon (10g) Dutch processed cocoa powder

¼ teaspoon kosher salt

¾ cup (150g) granulated sugar

¼ cup (53g) light brown sugar, packed

1 large egg, room temperature

1 teaspoon vanilla extract

1-2 teaspoon red gel food coloring

¼ cup (15g) graham cracker crumbs, for topping

FOR THE MARSHMALLOW

3 egg whites, room temperature

½ teaspoon cream of tartar

¾ cup (150g) granulated sugar

¼ cup (60ml) water

½ teaspoon vanilla extract

FOR THE GANACHE

½ cup (85g) milk chocolate chips

1 tablespoon heavy cream

1   Brown the butter by melting it in a small pan over medium heat. Cook the butter until it begins to turn a warm, golden amber color. Stir often and be careful not to let it burn. Browning the butter will take about 5 minutes. Let the brown butter cool completely.

2   In a medium bowl whisk together the all-purpose flour, baking powder, baking soda, cocoa powder, and salt. In a large bowl beat together the cooled brown butter, granulated sugar, and brown sugar on high until light and creamy, about two minutes. Add in the egg, vanilla, and 1-2 tsp of red gel food coloring (depending on how red you want your cookies) and mix on medium until combined. Sprinkle in the dry ingredients and mix on low until just combined. Be careful not to over mix. Scoop out 3-tablespoon sized cookie dough balls, roll them into balls, and place on the prepared parchment paper lined baking sheets. Use your hand to slightly flatten the cookie dough balls. Place the cookie dough in the fridge for 30 minutes to chill. During the last 15 minutes of chill time, preheat the oven to 350°F (175°C) and line two baking sheets with parchment paper. Bake 6 cookies at a time for 9-11 minutes.

3   While the cookies cool, make the marshmallow meringue. In a stand mixer, add the egg whites and cream of tartar. Beat together on medium high speed until soft peaks form. In a saucepan over medium heat, add the sugar and water and heat until it reaches a temperature of 240 degrees. Slowly pour the sugar water into the egg mixture at a low speed. Slowly increase the speed to high and mix until firm peaks form, for about 5-10 minutes. Once the firm peaks form, add in the vanilla extract and beat again on high. Transfer the meringue to a piping bag fitted with a decorative tip.

4   Make the chocolate fudge ganache by adding the chocolate chips to a microwave safe bowl. Pour the heavy cream over the chocolate and microwave for 45 seconds. Allow the mixture to sit for 1 minute before vigorously whisking to combine. Crush the graham crackers into small, fine crumbs and set aside. Assemble the cookies by spreading a layer of chocolate fudge ganache over the top of the cookie and sprinkle the graham cracker crumbs over the top of the fudge. Pipe the marshmallow meringue on top of the fudge. Using a blow torch, toast the marshmallow meringue until it's golden brown, this only takes about 1 second.

WHITE CHOCOLATE MATCHA LATTE COOKIES

MAKES 10 COOKIES

There are few better ways to start your morning than with a creamy white chocolate matcha latte. I love matcha so much, I decided to make it in cookie form! These matcha cookies are incredibly thick and soft with just the right amount of chew. Topped with a creamy, velvety white chocolate buttercream to balance out the earthiness of the matcha, these cookies will bring you the comforting warmth of your favorite, cozy matcha latte.

FOR THE COOKIES

1 2/3 cups (200g) all-purpose flour, spooned and leveled

½ teaspoon baking powder

½ teaspoon baking soda

1 tablespoon (5g) matcha powder, plus more for topping if desired

½ teaspoon kosher salt

½ cup (113g) unsalted butter, softened

¾ cup (150g) granulated sugar

¼ cup (53g) light brown sugar, packed

1 large egg, room temperature

1 teaspoon vanilla extract

FOR THE FROSTING

1 cup (170g) white chocolate chips, plus shaved white chocolate for topping

1 cup (226g) unsalted butter, softened

2 cups (240g) powdered sugar

1-3 tablespoons heavy cream

1 teaspoon vanilla extract

⅛ teaspoon kosher salt

1   In a medium bowl, whisk together the all-purpose flour, baking powder, baking soda, matcha powder, and salt. Set this aside.

2   In a large mixing bowl beat together the softened butter, granulated sugar, and brown sugar on high until light and fluffy. About two minutes. Add in the egg and vanilla extract and mix on medium until combined. Sprinkle in the dry ingredients and mix on low until just combined. Be careful not to over mix. Scoop out three tablespoon sized cookie dough balls, roll them into balls, and place on the prepared parchment paper lined baking sheets. Use your hand to slightly flatten the cookie dough balls. Place the cookie dough in the fridge for 30 minutes to chill. During the last 15 minutes of chill time, preheat the oven to 350°F (175°C) and line two baking sheets with parchment paper. Bake 6 cookies at a time for 9-11 minutes.

3   Make the white chocolate butter cream by adding the white chocolate chips to a microwave safe bowl. Microwave for 30 second increments, stirring in between, until smooth and melted. Allow this melted white chocolate to cool. In a mixing bowl, beat the softened butter on high until smooth. About 2-3 minutes. Reduce the speed to low, and add in the powdered sugar ½ cup at a time until fully mixed in. Add in the cooled, melted white chocolate, 1 tbsp of heavy cream, vanilla, and salt. Mix on medium until combined. If needed, add 1-2 more tbsp of heavy cream to achieve your desired consistency. Beat the buttercream on high for 1 minute until fluffy. Transfer the buttercream to a piping bag fitted with a decorative tip. Frost the cooled cookies with the white chocolate buttercream, sprinkle with matcha, and shaved white chocolate.

GRASSHOPPER MINT CHOCOLATE COOKIES

MAKES 12 COOKIES

Growing up, my mom would bring home grasshopper pies for us to enjoy for dessert. These grasshopper pies were frozen mint ice cream, speckled with chocolate chips, and topped with fudgy, chocolate ganache. This is where my love for mint chocolate began! What's better than a grasshopper pie? Mint chocolate pie in cookie form! With a thick, chewy chocolate cookie base, these are then topped with creamy, mint buttercream, decadent chocolate fudge ganache, and chocolate shavings.

FOR THE COOKIES

1½ cups (180g) all-purpose flour, spooned and leveled

½ cup (40g) Dutch processed cocoa powder

½ teaspoon baking powder

½ teaspoon kosher salt

¾ cup (170g) unsalted butter, softened

¾ cup (160g) light brown sugar, packed

¼ cup (50g) granulated sugar

2 large egg yolks, room temperature

1 teaspoon vanilla extract

½ teaspoon peppermint extract

Chocolate shavings for topping

FOR THE FROSTING

½ cup (113g) unsalted butter, softened

1 teaspoon vanilla extract

1 teaspoon peppermint extract

2-3 tablespoons heavy cream

2½ cups (270g) powdered sugar

1-4 drops green gel food coloring

FOR THE FUDGE

½ cup (85g) semi-sweet chocolate chips

1 tablespoon heavy cream

1   Preheat the oven to 350°F (175°C) and line two baking sheets with parchment paper. In a medium bowl whisk together the all-purpose flour, Dutch processed cocoa powder, baking powder, and salt. Set this aside. In a large mixing bowl, beat together the unsalted butter, light brown sugar, and granulated sugar on high until light and fluffy, about two minutes. Reduce the speed to medium and add in the egg yolks one at a time until fully incorporated. Add in the vanilla and peppermint extract and mix until combined. Sprinkle in the dry ingredients and mix until just combined. Be careful not to overmix. Scoop out 3 tbsp sized cookie dough balls, roll the cookie dough balls, and place them onto a baking sheet 2 inches apart. Press the cookie dough balls down slightly to flatten. Bake the cookies for 8-10 minutes. They will appear slightly doughy in the center but will continue to set as they cool.

2   While the cookies cool, make the mint buttercream. Beat the butter for 2 minutes on high speed until light and fluffy. Continuously scrape down the sides of the bowl. Add in the vanilla and peppermint extract on low speed. Slowly add in half of the powdered sugar. Add in 2 tbsp of heavy cream to make the mixing easier, then add in the remaining powdered sugar. If the frosting is too thick, add in the remaining 1 tbsp heavy cream. Beat on high for 1 minute. Add in the green gel food coloring and mix until the buttercream is fully green and smooth.

3   Make the chocolate fudge ganache by adding the chocolate chips to a microwave safe bowl. Pour the cream over the chocolate. Microwave for 45 seconds and allow the mixture to sit for 1 minute before vigorously whisking to combine. Assemble the cookies by spreading a layer of green mint buttercream over the whole top of the cookie. Add the remaining mint buttercream to a piping bag fitted with an open star decorating tip and pipe a border around the edge of the cookie. Fill the center of the cookie with the chocolate fudge ganache. Top with chocolate shavings if desired.

CHOCOLATE MALTED MILKSHAKE COOKIES

MAKES 10 COOKIES

Growing up, chocolate malted milkshakes were always my absolute favorite. Malted milk is one of the most deliciously underrated ingredients, and once you add it to any dessert, you'll understand just how incredible it is. These chocolate malted milkshake cookies are a thick and chewy chocolate malted cookie base, topped with creamy vanilla malted buttercream. Decorate them with a chocolate malted candy and a little straw, and they are just as delicious as they are cute.

FOR THE COOKIES

1½ cups (180g) all-purpose flour, spooned and leveled

⅓ cup (30g) Dutch processed cocoa powder

1 tablespoon (6g) malted milk powder

½ teaspoon baking powder

½ teaspoon kosher salt

¾ cup (170g) unsalted butter, softened

¾ cup (160g) light brown sugar, packed

¼ cup (50g) granulated sugar

2 large egg yolks, at room temperature

1½ teaspoon vanilla

10 chocolate malted milk balls for topping, if desired

FOR THE FROSTING

½ cup (113g) unsalted butter, softened

¼ teaspoon kosher salt

2½ cups (300g) powdered sugar

1 tablespoon (6g) malted milk powder

1-3 tablespoons heavy cream

1 teaspoon vanilla extract

FOR THE FUDGE GANACHE

½ cup (85g) semi-sweet chocolate chips

1 tablespoon heavy cream

1. Preheat the oven to 350°F (175°C) and line two baking sheets with parchment paper. In a medium bowl whisk together the flour, cocoa powder, malted milk powder, baking powder, and salt. Set this aside. In a large bowl, beat together on high the unsalted butter, light brown sugar, and granulated sugar until light and fluffy, about 2 minutes. Add in the two egg yolks and vanilla and mix on medium speed until combined. Sprinkle in the dry ingredients and mix on low until just combined. Scoop out three tablespoon sized cookie dough balls, roll them in your hands, and place them onto the prepared parchment line baking sheets. Flatten the cookie dough balls slightly. Bake 6 cookies at a time for 9-11 minutes until the edges are just slightly set.

2. While the cookies cool, make the malted vanilla buttercream. In a large bowl, beat together the softened butter and salt until light and fluffy. Add in the powdered sugar and malted milk powder and mix on low, slowly increasing the speed until combined. Add in 1 tbsp of heavy cream and vanilla extract. Mix to combine. If the frosting is too thick, add in an additional 1-2 tbsp of heavy cream. Transfer the buttercream to a piping bag fitted with a decorative tip.

3. Prepare the chocolate fudge ganache by adding the chocolate chips to a microwave safe bowl. Pour the heavy cream over the chocolate and microwave for 45 seconds. Let this mixture sit for 1 minute before vigorously whisking to combine. Assemble the chocolate malted milk shake cookies by spreading an even layer of chocolate fudge ganache over the top of the cookie. Pipe the malted vanilla buttercream over the top of the fudge ganache. Top the buttercream with a malted milk ball if desired.

COFFEE CRÈME BRÛLÉE SUGAR COOKIES

MAKES 12 COOKIES

If crème brûlée is on the menu, I am ordering it! I love how creamy and caramelized the dessert is, and I didn't think I could love it more until I made these coffee crème brûlée sugar cookies! With a soft, buttery coffee sugar cookie base, these are then topped with a velvety smooth coffee cream. The best part? The caramelized sugar on top crackles with every bite creating the most delicious contrast to the cream. Enjoy these coffee crème brûlée cookies with your post-dinner cappuccino for most decadent dessert.

FOR THE CRÈME

2 cups (473ml) whole milk

5 egg yolks

1 cup (200g) granulated sugar

¼ teaspoon kosher salt

1 teaspoon espresso powder

2 teaspoons vanilla extract

3 tablespoons cornstarch

3 tablespoons (43g) unsalted butter

FOR THE COOKIES

2½ cups (300g) all-purpose flour, spooned and leveled

½ teaspoon baking powder

1 tablespoon espresso powder

¼ teaspoon kosher salt

1 cup (227g) unsalted butter, softened

1¼ cups (250g) granulated sugar

1 large egg, room temperature

1 teaspoon vanilla extract

¼ cup (50g) granulated sugar, for the brûlée topping

FOR ROLLING

¼ cup (50g) granulated sugar

½ teaspoon espresso powder

1 Warm the milk in a saucepan until it's hot but not boiling. Keep it warm over low heat. In a separate bowl, mix the egg yolks, granulated sugar, salt, espresso powder, vanilla, and cornstarch until smooth and light in color. Slowly stir the warm milk into the mixture until it's well combined. Cook it in a saucepan over medium low heat until it thickens, stirring constantly. Remove the creamy mixture from heat, stir in the butter, cover it directly with plastic wrap, and put it in the fridge until it's cold.

2 Preheat the oven to 350°F (175°C) and line two baking sheets with parchment paper. Make the cookies by mixing the flour, baking powder, espresso powder, and salt in a bowl and set it aside. In a large mixing bowl, beat together the softened butter and granulated sugar until it is light and fluffy. About 2 minutes. Add the egg and vanilla to the butter mixture, beat until it's light and fluffy. Slowly add in the dry ingredients until a dough forms. In a small bowl, mix the sugar and espresso powder for rolling the cookie dough balls in. Set aside.

3 Scoop out 3 tbsp of dough, shape into balls, and coat them with the sugar and espresso powder mixture. Place them on the baking sheets, gently flatten, and bake for 8-10 minutes. Put the chilled pastry cream into a piping bag with a small tip. Once the cookies are cool, pipe pastry cream on top of each. Sprinkle sugar on the cream and use a kitchen blow torch to caramelize the sugar. Let the cookies cool a bit after torching before serving.

PEANUT BUTTER OREO SWIRL COOKIES

MAKES 12 COOKIES

It's a universal experience that we all watched the Parent Trap growing up and ran to our pantry to try Oreos dipped in peanut butter. Well, my life was forever changed. This has become one of my favorite flavor combinations, I just had to make it in cookie form! It starts with a chocolate cookie marbled together with a peanut butter cookie. With crushed Oreo pieces and melty chocolate dotted throughout, this cookie brings back all the nostalgia of watching that beloved movie for the first time!

FOR THE PEANUT BUTTER COOKIES

1 cup (120g) all-purpose flour, spooned and leveled

½ teaspoon baking powder

½ teaspoon baking soda

¾ teaspoon kosher salt

½ cup (113g) unsalted butter, softened

⅓ cup (67g) granulated sugar

½ cup (105g) light brown sugar, packed

½ cup (125g) peanut butter, I prefer Jif

1 large egg, room temperature

¾ teaspoon vanilla extract

FOR THE CHOCOLATE COOKIES

1⅓ cups (160g) all-purpose flour, spooned and leveled

⅓ cup (28g) Dutch processed cocoa powder

½ teaspoon baking soda

¼ teaspoon kosher salt

½ cup (113g) unsalted butter, softened

½ cup (105g) light brown sugar, packed

⅓ cup (67g) granulated sugar

1 large egg, room temperature

1 teaspoon vanilla extract

¾ cup (113g) semi-sweet chocolate chips, plus more for topping

¼ cup chopped Oreos, plus more for topping

1 Start by making the peanut butter dough. In a medium bowl, whisk together the all-purpose flour, baking powder, baking soda, and salt. Set this aside. In a large mixing bowl, beat together the butter, granulated sugar, and brown sugar until light and fluffy, about 2 minutes. Add in the peanut butter and mix on medium speed until combined. Add in the egg and vanilla, mixing on medium until incorporated. Scrape down the sides of the bowl. Sprinkle on the dry ingredients and mix on low until just combined. Chill the dough while you make the chocolate Oreo dough.

2 In a medium mixing bowl, whisk together the flour, cocoa powder, baking soda, and salt. Set this aside. In a large mixing bowl, beat together the butter, brown sugar, and granulated sugar until light and fluffy, about 2 minutes. Add the egg and vanilla and mix until combined. Sprinkle in the dry ingredients and mix on low until just combined. Be careful not to overmix. Fold in the semi-sweet chocolate chips and chopped Oreos with a rubber spatula. Cover the dough tightly and refrigerate with the peanut butter dough for 30 minutes.

3 During the last 15 minutes of chill time, preheat the oven to 350°F (175°C) and line two baking sheets with parchment paper. Using a 2 tbsp sized cookie dough scoop, scoop out a ball of each dough. Roll each ball of dough in your hands to form balls and then press them together, rolling again to form a ball. Bake 6 cookies at a time for 9-12 minutes. Top the cookies with extra chocolate chunks and chopped Oreo pieces.

FUNFETTI CAKE COOKIES

MAKES 12 COOKIES (OR 4 3-TIERED COOKIE CAKES)

Funfetti cake screams celebration to me! You don't need a birthday as an excuse to bake these rainbow sprinkle filled sugar cookie tiered cakes. Just as beautiful and delicious as a slice of Funfetti cake, without all the hassle and time spent in the kitchen. These chewy, rainbow sprinkle cookies are sandwiched with sweet, creamy buttercream and topped with more sprinkles.

FOR THE COOKIES

1⅓ cups (160g) all-purpose flour, spooned and leveled

1 teaspoon (2g) cornstarch

½ teaspoon baking soda

¼ teaspoon kosher salt

½ cup (113g) unsalted butter, softened

¼ cup (53g) light brown sugar, packed

½ cup (100g) granulated sugar

1 large egg yolk, room temperature

1 teaspoon vanilla extract

½ cup (80g) rainbow sprinkles, plus more for rolling

FOR THE FROSTING

½ cup (113g) unsalted butter, softened

2 cups (240g) powdered sugar

1 teaspoon vanilla extract

1 tablespoon heavy cream

¼ teaspoon kosher salt

1-3 drops light pink gel food coloring, or color of your choice

1 Preheat the oven to 350°F (175°C) and line two baking sheets with parchment paper. In a medium bowl, whisk together the all-purpose flour, cornstarch, baking soda, and salt. Set this aside. In a large mixing bowl, beat together the butter, brown sugar, and granulated sugar on high until light and creamy, about two minutes. Mix in the egg yolk and vanilla extract on medium speed until combined. Sprinkle in the dry ingredients and mix on low until just combined. Fold in the sprinkles. Add some extra sprinkles to a small bowl for rolling the dough if desired.

2 Scoop out 2 tablespoon size cookie dough balls and roll the tops of the cookie dough balls in the extra sprinkles. Place the cookie dough on the prepared baking sheets and bake for 8-10 minutes. Allow the cookies to sit on the baking tray for a few minutes before transferring them to a wire cooling rack to finish cooling completely.

3 While the cookies cool, make the buttercream frosting. In a mixing bowl, beat the butter on high for 3 minutes until completely smooth. If leaving the buttercream a white color, beat for an additional 2-3 minutes to make the butter less yellow. Slowly add in the powdered sugar ½ cup at a time until fully mixed in, beating on low. Add in the vanilla, heavy cream, and salt mixing on medium until combined. Mix in the food coloring and increase the speed to high for 1 minute until the buttercream is light and fluffy. Transfer the buttercream to a piping bag fitted with a decorative tip and frost the completely cooled cookies.

ESPRESSO BROWN BUTTER COOKIES WITH WHITE CHOCOLATE GLAZE

MAKES 10 COOKIES

Brown butter makes everything more delicious! It's warm, toasty, and adds the perfect amount of nuttiness to these thick, chewy espresso cookies. The freshly brewed espresso notes of these cookies are enhanced by the creamy, sweetness of the white chocolate glaze. It's like having your favorite morning coffee order for dessert!

FOR THE COOKIES

1 cup (227g) unsalted butter, browned

2 2/3 cups (320g) all-purpose flour, spooned and leveled

1 teaspoon baking soda

1 teaspoon kosher salt

1 tablespoon (6g) ground espresso powder, plus more for topping if desired

½ cup (100g) granulated sugar

½ cup (105g) light brown sugar, packed

1 large egg, room temperature

1 large egg yolk, room temperature

2 teaspoons vanilla extract

FOR THE GLAZE

½ cup (112g) white chocolate chips

¼ cup (60ml) milk

1 cup (120g) powdered sugar

1 To make the brown butter, melt the butter in a small saucepan over medium heat. Cook until dark amber, stirring often, about 5 minutes, and be careful not to let it burn. Allow the brown butter to fully cool.

2 In a medium bowl whisk together the flour, baking soda, salt, and ground espresso powder. Set this aside. In a large mixing bowl, beat together the granulated sugar, brown sugar, and cooled brown butter until a paste like texture forms. Add in the egg, egg yolk, and vanilla mixing on medium speed to combine. Sprinkle in the dry ingredients and mix on low until just combined. Cover the dough and transfer to the fridge for 30 minutes to chill.

3 During the last 15 minutes of chill time, preheat the oven to 350°F (175°C) and line two baking sheets with parchment paper. Using a 3-tablespoon sized cookie dough scoop, scoop out the cookie dough, roll in your hands to form perfect balls, and place on the prepared baking sheets. Bake six cookies at a time for 9 to 11 minutes until the edges are just slightly golden brown.

4 While the cookies cool, make the white chocolate glaze. Add the white chocolate chips and milk to a saucepan on medium low heat. Allow the white chocolate chips to melt, stirring regularly. Remove the saucepan from the heat and stir in the powdered sugar. Mix until the glaze is completely smooth. If a thicker, whiter glaze is desired, add more powdered sugar. Dip the cookies in the white chocolate glaze, place on parchment paper to set, and sprinkle with additional espresso powdered if desired.

UBE SUGAR COOKIES WITH
WHITE CHOCOLATE DRIZZLE

MAKES 10 COOKIES

The first time I tried ube, I fell in love! The creamy, yammy flavor is so unique and makes for the best addition to any dessert. These ube sugar cookies are loaded with ube flavor, rolled in sugar, and drizzled with creamy and melty white chocolate. Each cookie is soft, chewy and has the perfect balance of sweet, nutty ube and creamy, smooth white chocolate. These ube sugar cookies are just as delicious as they are beautiful!

FOR THE COOKIES

1 2/3 cups (200g) all-purpose flour, spooned and leveled

½ teaspoon baking powder

½ teaspoon baking soda

½ teaspoon kosher salt

3 tablespoons (12g) Ube powder

½ cup (113g) unsalted butter, softened

¾ cup (150g) granulated sugar, plus ⅓ cup (67g) for rolling

¼ cup (53g) light brown sugar, packed

1 large egg, room temperature

1 teaspoon vanilla extract

FOR THE DRIZZLE

½ cup (85g) white chocolate chips, melted

1. Preheat the oven to 350°F (175°C) and line two baking sheets with parchment paper. In a medium bowl, whisk together the all-purpose flour, baking powder, baking soda, salt, and Ube powder. Set this aside.

2. Using a stand mixer, beat together the butter, granulated sugar, and brown sugar until smooth. Add in the egg and vanilla extract and mix on medium low until combined. Sprinkle in the dry ingredients and mix on low until just combined. Scoop 3 tbsp sized balls of cookie dough, roll into perfect balls, and roll in the sugar before placing onto the prepared cookie sheets. Slightly press down the cookie dough balls before baking for 8-11 minutes. Allow the cookies to cool while you make the white chocolate drizzle.

3. Make the white chocolate drizzle by adding the white chocolate chips to a microwave safe bowl. Microwave at 30 second increments, stirring in between, until completely melted and smooth. Drizzle the white chocolate on top of the cooled cookies and allow the chocolate to set for 5 minutes before serving.

S'MORES SANDWICH COOKIES

MAKES 10 S'MORES SANDWICH COOKIES

S'mores are the ultimate summertime dessert to enjoy around a bonfire on a warm, starry night. These s'more sandwich cookies are thick and chewy graham cracker cookies stuffed with a layer of creamy chocolate fudge ganache and toasted marshmallow meringue. Your favorite summertime dessert, in cookie form!

FOR THE COOKIES

1 2/3 cups (200g) all-purpose flour, spooned and leveled

½ teaspoon baking powder

½ teaspoon baking soda

½ teaspoon kosher salt

⅓ cup (22g) graham cracker crumbs, about 1½ sheets

½ cup (113g) unsalted butter, softened

¾ cup (150g) granulated sugar

¼ cup (53g) light brown sugar, packed

1 large egg, room temperature

1 teaspoon vanilla extract

FOR THE CHOCOALTE

½ cup (85g) milk chocolate chips

1 tablespoon heavy cream

FOR THE MARSHMALLOW

3 egg whites, room temperature

½ teaspoon cream of tartar

¾ cup (150g) granulated sugar

¼ cup (60ml) water

½ teaspoon vanilla extract

1. Preheat the oven to 350°F (175°C) and line two baking sheets with parchment paper. In a medium bowl, whisk together the all-purpose flour, baking powder, baking soda, salt, and graham cracker crumbs. Set this aside. Using a stand mixer, beat together the butter, granulated sugar, and brown sugar until smooth. Add the egg and vanilla and mix on medium low until combined. Scoop 3 tbsp sized balls of cookie dough, roll into perfect balls, and place onto the prepared cookie sheets. Bake for 9-11 minutes until the edges are slightly golden brown.

2. While the cookies cool, prepare the milk chocolate ganache. Add the milk chocolate chips to a microwave safe bowl, pour the heavy cream over the chocolate, and microwave for 45 seconds. Allow the chocolate ganache to sit for one minute before vigorously whisking. Assemble the s'mores sandwiches by spreading a thick layer of chocolate ganache on the bottom of one graham cracker cookie. Transfer the cookies with the fudge layer to the fridge for 10 minutes while you make the marshmallow frosting.

3. In a stand mixer, add the egg whites and cream of tartar. Beat together on medium high speed until soft peaks form. In a saucepan over medium heat, add the sugar and water and heat until it reaches a temperature of 240 degrees. Slowly pour the sugar water into the egg mixture on low speed. Slowly increase the speed to high and mix until firm peaks form, for about 5-10 minutes. Once the firm peaks form, add in the vanilla extract and beat again on high. Transfer the marshmallow meringue to a piping bag fitted with a decorative tip. Pipe the marshmallow meringue over the chocolate ganache. Using a blow torch, torch the marshmallow meringue until toasty and golden. Add a second graham cracker cookie on top of the marshmallow meringue.

TWIX COOKIES

MAKES 12 COOKIES

These twix shortbread sugar cookies are one of my favorite cookies in the whole book, and I know they will be your favorite too! It all starts with the most buttery, delicious shortbread sugar cookie topped with a rich layer of creamy caramel and milk chocolate on top. With chopped twix cookies and flaky sea salt in every bite, there are not enough words to describe how delicious these cookies are!

FOR THE COOKIES

2½ cups (300g) all-purpose flour, spooned and leveled

½ teaspoon baking powder

½ teaspoon kosher salt

1 cup (227g) unsalted butter, softened

1 cup (200g) granulated sugar

1 large egg yolk, room temperature

1½ teaspoons vanilla extract

5 mini Twix bars, chopped

Flaky sea salt for topping, if desired

FOR THE CARAMEL

10 ounces caramels, unwrapped

1 tablespoon heavy cream

FOR THE CHOCOLATE

1 cup (170g) milk chocolate chips

1 Preheat the oven to 350°F (175°C) and line two baking sheets with parchment paper. In a medium bowl, whisk together the all-purpose flour, baking powder, and salt. Set this aside. In a large bowl, beat together the butter and granulated sugar on high until light and fluffy, about 2 minutes. Add in the egg yolk and vanilla and mix on medium speed until the mixture turns a pale color, about 1 minute. Sprinkle in the dry ingredients and mix on low until just combined. Continuously scrape down the sides as needed. Using a 3-tablespoon sized cookie dough scoop, scoop out cookie dough balls, roll them in your hands, and place them on the prepared baking sheets. Press them down with your hand to flatten them slightly. Bake for 9-11 minutes until the edges start to turn just slightly golden. The centers will look doughy, the cookies will continue to set as they cool. After 5 minutes of setting on the baking sheets, transfer the cookies to a wire cooling rack to continue setting.

2 While the cookies cool, make the caramel sauce by adding the unwrapped caramels to a microwave safe bowl, and pour the cream over the top. Microwave at 30 second increments, stirring until smooth and fully melted. Work quickly to spread an even layer of caramel sauce over the whole top of each cookie. If the sauce starts to get hard to work with, microwave for an additional 10-15 seconds. Place the cookies in the fridge to allow the caramel layer to set for 10 minutes while you prepare the melted chocolate.

3 Add the milk chocolate chips to a microwave safe bowl and microwave at 30 second increments, stirring until smooth and fully melted. Spread the melted chocolate on top of the caramel layer. Top the cookies with chopped Twix bars and flaky sea salt.

DIRT AND WORM COOKIES

MAKES 12 COOKIES

Dirt and Worm Cookies take me right back to my childhood, when I loved digging into the classic dirt and worms dessert. These cookies are a fun twist on that nostalgic treat, with a soft, chewy chocolate base topped with crushed cookie "dirt" and gummy worms wriggling on top. Growing up, the mix of rich chocolate and sweet gummy worms was always a favorite, and now these cookies bring that playful combo to life in a delicious, bite-sized form. Perfect for parties or when you want a fun, nostalgic dessert, they're sure to be a hit for kids and adults alike!

FOR THE COOKIES

1½ cups (188g) all-purpose flour, spooned and leveled

½ cup (40g) Dutch processed cocoa powder

½ teaspoon baking powder

½ teaspoon kosher salt
¾ cup (170g) unsalted butter, softened

¾ cup (160g) light brown sugar, packed

¼ cup (50g) granulated white sugar

2 egg yolks, room temperature

1 teaspoon vanilla extract

FOR THE FROSTING

½ cup (113g) unsalted butter, softened

2½ cups (284g) powdered sugar

⅓ cup (28g) cocoa powder

1-3 tablespoons heavy cream

1 teaspoon vanilla extract

¼ teaspoon salt

½ cup crushed Oreos, chocolate cookie and frosting filling

FOR TOPPING

⅛ cup crushed Oreos, chocolate cookie and frosting filling

12 gummy worms, one for each cookie

1 Preheat the oven to 350°F (175°C) and line two baking sheets with parchment paper. In a medium bowl, whisk together the flour, cocoa powder, baking powder, and salt. Set this aside. In a large mixing bowl, beat together the butter, brown sugar, and granulated sugar until light and fluffy, about 2 minutes. Reduce the speed to medium low and add in the egg yolks one at a time until fully incorporated. Mix in the vanilla. Gradually add in the dry ingredients and mix on low until just combined. Using a 3 tbsp sized cookie dough scoop, scoop out 12 cookie dough balls and place on the prepared baking sheets. Bake for 9-11 minutes until the edges are starting to set.

2 Meanwhile, prepare the chocolate buttercream. In a large bowl, beat together the softened butter until light and fluffy. Add in the powdered sugar and cocoa powder and mix on low slowly increasing the speed until combined. Add in 1 tbsp of the heavy cream, vanilla extract, and salt. Add in 1-2 more tbsp of heavy cream to achieve your desired consistency. Beat the buttercream on high for 1 minute until fluffy. Using a rubber spatula, fold in the crushed Oreo cookies. Assemble the cookies by spreading an even layer of the chocolate buttercream on each cooled cookie. Top the cookies with crushed Oreos and a gummy worm and enjoy!

CHURRO COOKIES WITH CINNAMON BUTTERCREAM

MAKES 12 COOKIES

This Churro Cookie is a cinnamon lover's dream, blending the soft, chewy texture of a cookie with the sweet, spiced flavor of a classic churro. Topped with a smooth and creamy cinnamon buttercream, it delivers a perfect balance of warmth and sweetness in every bite. The cinnamon sugar-dusted cookie paired with the rich buttercream creates a treat that's indulgent, comforting, and irresistibly delicious, making it the perfect dessert for any churro fan.

FOR ROLLING

½ cup (100g) granulated sugar

1 tablespoon cinnamon

FOR THE COOKIES

2¾ cups (330g) all-purpose flour, spooned and leveled

1 teaspoon baking soda

1 teaspoon baking powder

½ teaspoon kosher salt

2 teaspoons cinnamon

½ teaspoon nutmeg

¼ teaspoon ground cloves

1 cup (226g) unsalted butter, softened

¾ cup (150g) granulated sugar

¾ cup (160g) light brown sugar, packed

2 eggs, room temperature

1 teaspoon vanilla extract

FOR THE BUTTERCREAM

½ cup (113g) unsalted butter, softened

2 cups (225g) powdered sugar

¼ cup (53g) light brown sugar, packed

1 teaspoon cinnamon

1 teaspoon vanilla extract

1-3 tablespoons heavy cream

1 Preheat the oven to 350°F (175°C) and line two baking sheets with parchment paper. Mix together the rolling ingredients and set aside while you make the cookies. In a medium bowl, whisk together the flour, baking soda, baking powder, salt, cinnamon, nutmeg, and ground cloves. Set this aside

2 In a large mixing bowl, beat together the butter, granulated sugar, and brown sugar on high until light and fluffy, about 2 minutes. Add in the eggs one at a time until fully incorporated, followed by the vanilla. Reduce the speed to low and gradually add in the dry ingredients until just mixed in. Scoop out 3 tbsp sized cookie dough balls, roll them in the cinnamon sugar, and place on the prepared baking sheets. Bake for 9-11 minutes and allow to fully cool while you make the buttercream.

3 In a large mixing bowl, beat the softened butter on high for 3-4 minutes until completely smooth. Reduce the speed to low and add in the powdered sugar ½ cup at a time until fully mixed in. Add in the brown sugar, cinnamon, vanilla, and 1 tbsp heavy cream. If needed, add in 1-2 more tbsp heavy cream to achieve your desired consistency. Beat the buttercream on high for 1 minute until fluffy. Transfer the buttercream to a piping bag fitted with a decorative tip. Forst the cooled cookies and enjoy!

HOLIDAY COOKIES

CHAMPAGNE SUGAR COOKIES

MAKES 10 COOKIES

Pop the champagne bottles and bake yourself a batch of these festive, sparkly champagne sugar cookies to ring in the new year! With a chewy sugar cookie base, these cookies are topped with sweet, champagne buttercream, and sparkly gold sprinkles. Add a real life sparkler to the cookies for a show stopping dessert at your NYE party. They are so festive and will wow all of your guests!

FOR THE COOKIES

2¾ cups (330g) all-purpose flour, spooned and leveled

1 teaspoon baking soda

½ teaspoon baking powder

½ teaspoon kosher salt

1 cup (227g) unsalted butter, softened

1 cup (200g) granulated sugar

½ cup (105g) light brown sugar, packed

1 large egg, room temperature

1 egg yolk, room temperature

1 teaspoon vanilla extract

Gold sprinkles for topping

FOR THE FROSTING

½ cup (113g) unsalted butter, softened

2½ cups (300g) powdered sugar

2-4 tablespoons champagne or sparkling wine

½ teaspoon vanilla extract

¼ teaspoon kosher salt

1. In a medium bowl, whisk together the all-purpose flour, baking soda, baking powder, and salt. Set this aside. In a large mixing bowl, beat together the softened butter, granulated sugar, and light brown sugar until the mixture is light and fluffy, about 2 minutes. Beat in the egg and egg yolk one at a time, mixing well after each addition. Add the vanilla extract and mix until fully incorporated. Gradually add the dry ingredients to the wet ingredients, mixing on low speed until just combined. Be careful not to overmix the dough. Cover the dough and chill in the refrigerator for at least 30 minutes. During the last 15 minutes of chill time, preheat the oven to 350°F (175°C) and line two baking sheets with parchment paper.

2. Using a 3 tbsp sized cookie scoop, drop rounded spoonfuls of dough onto the prepared baking sheets, spacing them about 2 inches apart. Bake for 10-12 minutes, or until the edges are lightly golden but the centers are still soft and pale. The cookies will continue to firm up as they cool. Allow the cookies to cool on the baking sheet for 5 minutes before transferring them to a wire rack to cool completely.

3. While the cookies cool, make the champagne buttercream. Beat the softened butter on high until light and fluffy. About two minutes. Slowly add in the powdered sugar and beat on low, increasing the speed to high for about one minute until combined. Add in 2 tbsp of champagne, vanilla extract, and salt and mixed to combine. Add an additional 1-2 tbsp of champagne if desired for a thinner frosting consistency. Transfer the frosting to a piping bag fitted with a decorated tip. Frost the cool cookies with the champagne buttercream and top with gold sprinkles.

LUCKY CHARMS SUGAR COOKIES

MAKES 12 COOKIES

A fun twist on a nostalgic cereal, these lucky charms sugar cookies are the most delicious cookie to bake up! With a chewy sugar cookie base, these are frosted with cereal milk buttercream and topped with a generous helping of marshmallows and cereal. Perfect for St. Paddy's Day, or any day of the year, you can be young or old to enjoy a lucky charms sugar cookie!

FOR THE COOKIES

2½ cups (300g) all-purpose flour, spooned and leveled

½ teaspoon baking powder

¼ teaspoon kosher salt

1 cup (227g) unsalted butter, softened

1¼ cups (250g) granulated sugar

1 large egg, room temperature

1 teaspoon vanilla extract

½ cup lucky charms cereal, for topping

FOR THE FROSTING

¼ cup lucky charms cereal

¼ cup milk

1 cup (226g) unsalted butter, softened

2 cups (240g) powdered sugar

1 teaspoon vanilla extract

⅛ teaspoon kosher salt

1 Preheat the oven to 350°F (175°C) and line two baking sheets with parchment paper. In a medium bowl, whisk the all-purpose flour, baking powder, and salt and set it aside. In a large mixing bowl, beat together the softened butter and granulated sugar until it is light and fluffy, about 2 minutes. Add in the egg and vanilla and mix until fully incorporated. Slowly add and mix in the dry ingredients until a dough forms. Do not overmix.

2 Using a 3 tbsp sized cookie dough scoop, scoop out the cookie dough balls, place them on the baking sheets, and bake for 9-11 minutes. Let the cookies cool on the baking sheet before transferring them to a cooling rack. While the cookies cool, make the cereal milk buttercream.

3 In a small bowl, add the milk and cereal together and let sit while you start the frosting. In a mixing bowl, beat the butter on high until completely smooth, about 3 minutes. Reduce the speed to low and add in the powdered sugar ½ cup at a time until fully combined. Strain the cereal milk and add it to the mixing bowl with the vanilla and salt. Beat on medium until it comes together, increasing the speed to high for 1 minute. Transfer the buttercream to a piping bag fitted with a piping tip. Assemble the cookies by frosting an even layer of buttercream over the top of the cookie. Top with lucky charms cereal.

EASTER EGG SUGAR COOKIES

MAKES 12 COOKIES

There's nothing I love more than beautiful, pastel milk chocolate eggs during the springtime. These chewy, sweet sugar cookies are frosted with the most beautiful robin's egg blue buttercream and topped with mini milk chocolate eggs. There's nothing cuter and more springtime than this! Make up a batch of these beautiful sugar cookies for your Easter dessert table.

FOR THE COOKIES

1½ cups (180g) all-purpose flour

¼ teaspoon salt

¾ teaspoon baking powder

¼ teaspoon baking soda

½ cup (113g) unsalted butter, softened

⅓ cup (67g) granulated sugar

3 tablespoons (23g) powdered sugar

1 large egg, room temperature

½ teaspoon vanilla extract

½ teaspoon almond extract

¼ cup milk chocolate eggs, for topping

FOR THE FROSTING

1 cup (226g) unsalted butter, softened

2 cups (240g) powdered sugar

1-3 tablespoons heavy cream

1 teaspoon vanilla extract

⅛ teaspoon kosher salt

1-3 drops light blue gel food coloring

1 Preheat the oven to 350°F (175°C) and line two baking sheets with parchment paper. In a medium bowl, whisk together the flour, salt, baking powder, and baking soda. Set this aside. In a large mixing bowl, beat together the butter, granulated sugar, and powdered sugar until light and fluffy, about 2 minutes. Add in the egg, vanilla, and almond extract mixing on medium speed until fully combined. Sprinkle in the dry ingredients and mix on low until just combined. Do not overmix.

2 Use a 2-tablespoon sized cookie dough scoop to scoop out the cookie dough. Roll it between your hand to form a circle, place it on the prepared baking sheets, and press down to slightly flatten the cookie dough balls. Bake for 9-11 minutes.

3 While the cookies cool, make the buttercream. In a mixing bowl, beat the butter on high until it is light and smooth, about 2 minutes. Reduce the speed and add in the powdered sugar ½ cup at a time until combined. Add in 1 tbsp heavy cream, vanilla extract, salt, and food coloring mixing on medium speed until smooth. If needed, add in 1-2 more tbsp of heavy cream to achieve your desired consistency. Beat on high for 1 minute until fluffy. Transfer the buttercream to a piping bag fitted with a decorative tip. Assemble the cookies by piping an even layer of buttercream over each cookie. Pipe on a circle of buttercream in the center of the cookie to make a nest for the chocolate eggs. Top the buttercream nest with a few chocolate eggs.

CARROT CAKE COOKIES WITH SPICED CHAI FROSTING

MAKES 10 COOKIES

Carrot cake has always been one of my favorite flavors, and it doesn't have to be Easter for you to enjoy these carrot cake inspired cookies topped with creamy chai buttercream frosting! Each bite is loaded with chewy carrot and spiced to perfection. Topped with crunchy walnuts, these cookies will be the star of your Easter dessert table.

FOR THE COOKIES

1¾ cups (210g) all-purpose flour, spooned and leveled

2 tablespoons (16g) cornstarch

½ teaspoon baking soda

½ teaspoon kosher salt

½ teaspoon cinnamon

¼ teaspoon ginger

⅛ teaspoon nutmeg

¾ cup (75g) finely grated carrots

½ cup (113g) unsalted butter, softened

¾ cup (160g) light brown sugar, packed

1 large egg, room temperature

½ teaspoon vanilla extract

¼ cup chopped walnuts, if desired

FOR THE FROSTING

4 ounces (112g) cream cheese, softened

4 tablespoons (56g) unsalted butter, softened

2½ cups (300g) powdered sugar

½ teaspoon vanilla extract

¼ teaspoon kosher salt

½ teaspoon ground cinnamon

¼ teaspoon ground ginger

⅛ teaspoon ground cardamom
⅛ teaspoon ground nutmeg

⅛ teaspoon ground cloves

⅛ teaspoon ground allspice

1. Preheat the oven to 350°F (175°C) and line two baking sheets with parchment paper. In a medium bowl, whisk together the all-purpose flour, cornstarch, baking soda, salt, cinnamon, ginger, and nutmeg. Set this aside.

2. Grate the carrots into a cheese cloth and ring out the excess carrot juice. In a large mixing bowl, beat together the butter and brown sugar until light and fluffy, about 2 minutes. Add in the egg and vanilla extract and mix on medium until combined. Slowly add in the dry ingredients, mixing on low until just combined. Using a rubber spatula, fold in the carrots and chopped walnuts. Scoop 3 tbsp sized balls of cookie dough onto a cookie sheet and bake for 8-10 minutes until the tops of the cookies are slightly golden brown. Allow the cookies to cool while you make the spiced chai cream cheese frosting.

3. Beat together the cream cheese and butter until light and fluffy (about 3-4 minutes). Reduce the speed and add in the powdered sugar ½ cup at a time until fully combined. Mix in the vanilla, salt, cinnamon, ginger, cardamom, nutmeg, cloves, and all spice until combined. Beat on high for 1 minute until fluffy. Transfer the chai spiced cream cheese frosting to a piping bag fitted with a decorative tip. Frost the cookies and top them with additional chopped walnuts.

FROSTED PUMPKIN CAKE COOKIES

MAKES 12 COOKIES

Once the leaves start to turn golden, I want all the pumpkin treats! Theses cookies are a pumpkin lovers' dream. With a soft and fluffy pumpkin cake cookie topped with a delicious swirl of decadent cream cheese frosting, these cookies are the perfect autumn treat to bake up on the first chilly day of fall.

FOR THE COOKIES

½ cup (122g) pumpkin puree

1¾ cups (210g) all-purpose flour, spooned and leveled

1 tablespoon pumpkin pie spice, plus more for garnishing

½ teaspoon baking powder

½ teaspoon baking soda

½ teaspoon kosher salt

¾ cup (170g) unsalted butter, softened

1 cup (210g) light brown sugar, packed

2 large egg yolks, room temperature

1½ teaspoons vanilla

FOR THE FROSTING

4 ounces (112g) cream cheese, softened

¼ cup (57g) unsalted butter, softened

1½ cups (360g) powdered sugar

1 teaspoon vanilla extract

⅛ teaspoon kosher salt

1 Preheat the oven to 350°F (175°C) and line two baking sheets with parchment paper. Using a cheesecloth, squeeze the excess water out of the pumpkin puree. Set aside. In a bowl, whisk together the flour, pumpkin pie spice, baking powder, baking soda, and salt. Set this mixture aside.

2 In a large mixing bowl, beat together the butter and brown sugar for 2-3 minutes until fluffy and combined. Add in the egg yolks one at a time until mixed in. Add in the vanilla and pumpkin puree and mix until combined. Sprinkle in the dry ingredients and mix on low speed until just combined. Do not overmix. Using a 3 tbsp sized cookie dough scoop, scoop out the cookies, place on the parchment lined baking sheets, and bake for 9-11 minutes. While the cookies cool on a wire cooling rack, make the cream cheese frosting.

3 Beat together the cream cheese and butter on high speed until smooth and fluffy. Add in the powdered sugar, vanilla, and salt and beat on low speed while slowly increasing the speed to high for 2 minutes. Transfer the frosting to a piping bag. Swirl the frosting onto each cooled, pumpkin cookie. Sprinkle on pumpkin pie spice over the frosting swirl.

CANDY CORN PEANUT BUTTER HARVEST COOKIES

MAKES 10 COOKIES

You either love it or hate it: Candy corn. I am a candy corn lover, and these cookies are packed full of all the festive flavors of fall! Salty peanuts, crunchy pretzels, creamy chocolate and peanut butter chips, and sweet and chewy candy corn make for the most nostalgic fall treat. It's like a harvest fall trail mix packed into one, incredibly delicious cookie!

1 cup (120g) all-purpose flour, spooned and leveled

½ teaspoon baking powder

½ teaspoon baking soda

¾ teaspoon kosher salt

½ cup (113g) unsalted butter, softened

⅓ cup (67g) granulated sugar

½ cup (105g) light brown sugar, packed

½ cup (125g) peanut butter, full sugar like Jif or Skippy (not natural)

1 large egg, room temperature

¾ teaspoon vanilla extract

¼ cup (43g) semi-sweet chocolate chips

¼ cup (43g) peanut butter chips

¼ cup (30g) pretzels, roughly chopped

¼ cup (35g) peanuts, roughly chopped

¼ cup (43g) Reese's pieces

¼ cup (30g) candy corn, for topping

1 Preheat the oven to 350°F (175°C) and line two baking sheets with parchment paper. In a medium bowl, whisk together the all-purpose flour, baking powder, baking soda, and salt. Set this aside.

2 In a large mixing bowl, beat together the butter, granulated sugar, and brown sugar until light and fluffy, for about 2 minutes. Add the peanut butter and mix on medium speed until combined. Add the egg and vanilla, mixing on medium until incorporated. Scrape down the sides of the bowl. Sprinkle on the dry ingredients and mix on low until just combined. Using a rubber spatula, fold in the semi-sweet chocolate chips, peanut butter chips, chopped pretzels, chopped peanuts, and Reese's pieces into the dough.

3 Using a 3 tbsp sized cookie dough scoop, scoop out a ball of each dough and place on the prepared baking sheets. Bake 6 cookies at a time for 9-12 minutes. Out of the oven, top the cookies with the candy corn.

CINNAMON STREUSEL COFFEE CAKE COOKIES

MAKES 10 COOKIES

There's nothing more heartwarming than a thick slice of warm coffee cake paired with a mug of coffee in the morning. These coffee cake cookies bring all the delicious flavors of coffee cake, in cookie form! Topped with buttery, cinnamon streusel and a vanilla glaze, these cookies are moist, chewy, and melt in your mouth.

FOR THE STREUSEL

¼ cup (50g) granulated sugar

¼ cup (53g) light brown sugar, packed

½ cup (60g) all-purpose flour, spooned and leveled

½ teaspoon cinnamon

4 tablespoons (57g) unsalted butter, softened

FOR THE ROLLING

1 cup (200g) granulated sugar

1½ teaspoons cinnamon

FOR THE COOKIES

2½ cups (300g) all-purpose flour, spooned and leveled

½ teaspoon kosher salt

½ teaspoon baking powder

½ teaspoon cinnamon

1 cup (227g) unsalted butter, softened

1 cup (200g) granulated sugar

1 large egg yolk, room temperature

1 teaspoon vanilla extract

FOR THE VANILLA ICING

½ cup (60g) powdered sugar

1-2 tablespoons milk

¼ teaspoon vanilla extract

1 Make the streusel by adding the granulated sugar, brown sugar, all-purpose flour, and cinnamon to a small bowl. Stir in the softened butter, then use your hands to mix all the ingredients until a crumb like texture forms. Set this aside. Preheat the oven to 350°F (175°C) and line two baking sheets with parchment paper. In a small bowl, mix the sugar and cinnamon for rolling and set aside.

2 Make the cookies. In a medium bowl, whisk together the flour, salt, baking powder, and cinnamon. Set aside. In a large bowl, beat together the butter and granulated sugar on high until light and fluffy, about 2 minutes. Add in the egg yolk and vanilla extract and mix on medium speed until the mixture turns a pale color, about 1 minute. Sprinkle in the dry ingredients and mix on low until just combined. Continuously scrape down the sides as needed. Using a 3-tablespoon sized cookie dough scoop, scoop out cookie dough balls, roll them in your hands, and place them on the prepared baking sheets. Press them down with your hand to flatten them slightly. Add about 1 tsp of streusel to the top of each cookie dough.

3 Bake for 9-11 minutes until the edges start to turn just slightly golden. In a small bowl, make the vanilla icing by mixing the powdered sugar, milk, and vanilla extract. Drizzle the icing on top of the cooled cookies and enjoy!

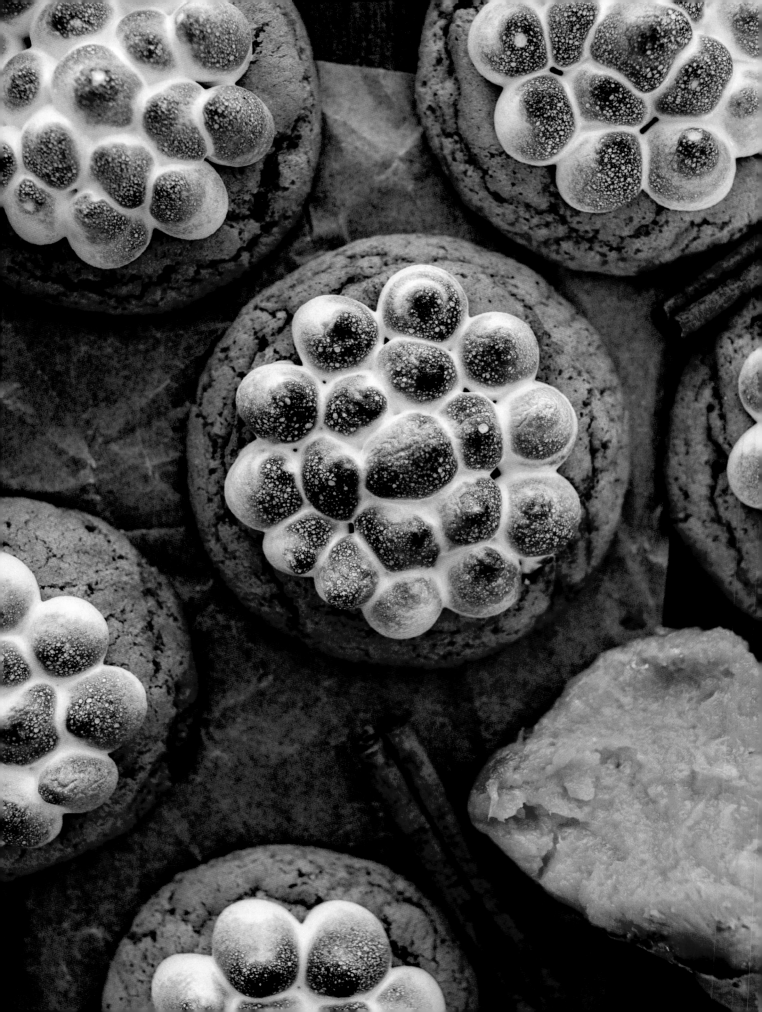

SWEET POTATO TOASTED MARSHMALLOW COOKIES

MAKES 10 COOKIES

The age-old debate! Do marshmallows belong on sweet potato casserole? Whether you are team marshmallows or against, you're sure to enjoy these sweet potato cookies with toasted marshmallow meringue! Each chewy, warm sweet potato cookie is topped with fluffy, sweet marshmallow meringue. Once torched, these cookies are melty, toasty and the perfect treat to serve on your Thanksgiving dessert table.

FOR THE COOKIES

¼ cup (66g) mashed sweet potato

½ cup (113g) unsalted butter, browned and cooled

2 cups (240g) all-purpose flour, spooned and leveled

¾ teaspoon baking soda

½ teaspoon kosher salt

2 teaspoons cinnamon

¼ teaspoon ginger

⅛ teaspoon nutmeg

⅛ teaspoon ground cloves

1 cup (210g) light brown sugar, packed

1 large egg, room temperature

1½ teaspoons vanilla extract

FOR THE MARSHMALLOW

3 egg whites, room temperature

½ teaspoon cream of tartar

¾ cup (150g) granulated sugar

¼ cup (60ml) water

½ teaspoon vanilla extract

1 Preheat the oven to 420°F (215°C) and line a baking sheet with foil. Bake a small sweet potato for 40-50 minutes, until soft. On a plate, mash ¼ cup of the sweet potato and set aside to cool. Brown the butter by melting it in a small pan over medium heat. Cook the butter until it begins to turn a warm, golden amber color. Stir often and be careful not to let it burn. Browning the butter will take about 5 minutes. Let the brown butter cool completely.

2 In a medium bowl whisk together the all-purpose flour, baking soda, salt, cinnamon, ginger, nutmeg, and ground cloves. Set aside. In a large bowl beat together the cooled brown butter and brown sugar on medium speed until fully combined. Add in the egg and vanilla and mix on medium until combined. Add in the mashed sweet potato and mix until combined. Sprinkle in the dry ingredients and mix on low until just combined. Be careful not to over mix. Cover the dough and place it in the fridge to chill for 1 hour. During the last 15 minutes of chill time, preheat the oven to 350°F (175°C) and line two baking sheets with parchment paper.

3 While the cookie dough chills, make the marshmallow meringue. In a stand mixer, add the egg whites and cream of tartar. Beat together on medium high speed until soft peaks form. In a saucepan over medium heat, add the sugar and water and heat until it reaches a temperature of 240°F (115°C). Slowly pour the sugar water into the egg mixture on low speed. Slowly increase the speed to high and mix until firm peaks form, for about 5-10 minutes. Once the firm peaks form, add in the vanilla extract and beat again on high. Transfer the marshmallow meringue to a piping bag fitted with a decorative tip.

4 Scoop out three tablespoon sized cookie dough balls, roll them into balls, and place on the prepared parchment paper lined baking sheets and bake for 9-11 minutes. Assemble the cookies by piping the marshmallow meringue on top of the cookies. Using a blow torch, toast the marshmallow meringue until it's golden brown, this only takes about 1 second.

PECAN PIE CHEESECAKE COOKIES

MAKES 10 COOKIES

These ooey gooey pecan pie cheesecake cookies are one of the most delicious things in the world. The chewy, graham cracker cookie base is frosted with a velvety cream cheese frosting and topped with sticky, indulgent pecan pie filling. These cookies have all the flavor of a pecan pie, in adorable individual sized dessert! Bake up a batch for your thanksgiving table for a fun and festive twist on a classic holiday dessert.

FOR THE COOKIES

1 2/3 cups (200g) all-purpose flour, spooned and leveled

½ teaspoon baking powder

½ teaspoon baking soda

½ teaspoon kosher salt

¼ cup (15g) graham cracker crumbs, about 1 sheet

½ cup (113g) unsalted butter, softened

¾ cup (150g) granulated sugar

¼ cup (53g) light brown sugar, packed

1 large egg, room temperature

1 teaspoon vanilla extract

FOR THE FROSTING

4 ounces (112g) cream cheese, softened

4 tablespoons (56g) unsalted butter, softened

2½ cups (300g) powdered sugar

½ teaspoon vanilla extract

¼ teaspoon kosher salt

FOR THE PECAN TOPPING

¾ cup (90g) pecans roughly chopped

⅛ cup (40g) light corn syrup

3 tablespoons (38g) light brown sugar, packed

3 tablespoons (45g) heavy cream

½ teaspoon cinnamon

2 tablespoons (28g) unsalted butter

¼ teaspoon kosher salt

½ teaspoon vanilla extract

1   Preheat the oven to 350°F (175°C) and line two baking sheets with parchment paper. In a medium bowl, whisk together the all-purpose flour, baking powder, baking soda, salt, and the food processed graham cracker crumbs. Set this aside.

2   Using a stand mixer, beat together the butter, granulated sugar, and brown sugar until smooth. Add in the egg and vanilla extract and mix on medium low until combined. Sprinkle in the dry ingredients and mix on low until just combined. Scoop 3 tbsp sized balls of cookie dough, roll into perfect balls, and place onto the prepared cookie sheets. Bake for 9-11 minutes until the edges are slightly golden brown. Allow the cookies to cool while you make the cream cheese frosting.

3   Beat together the cream cheese and butter until light and fluffy (about 3-4 minutes). Slowly add in the powdered sugar and beat on low until all combined. Add in the vanilla extract and salt. Scoop the cream cheese frosting into a piping bag and frost the cookies.

4   To prepare the pecan topping, combine the chopped pecans, light corn syrup, light brown sugar, heavy cream, cinnamon, unsalted butter, and salt in a medium saucepan over medium heat. Bring the mixture to a gentle boil, stirring constantly, then reduce the heat and simmer for 4-5 minutes until it thickens slightly. Remove the saucepan from the heat and stir in the vanilla extract. Once done, pour the pecan pie topping over the cream cheese frosting layer.

WHITE CHOCOLATE PEPPERMINT CHEESECAKE COOKIES

MAKES 10 COOKIES

These white chocolate peppermint cheesecake sugar cookies bring together the festive flavors of the holiday season in one irresistible treat. The base is a soft, buttery peppermint sugar cookie topped with creamy peppermint cream cheese frosting. The crunch of the crushed candy cane on top will get you in the Christmas spirit! Enjoy these white chocolate peppermint cheesecake sugar cookies with a warm mug of hot cocoa by the fire while you hang your stockings for Santa.

FOR THE COOKIES

2¾ cups (330g) all-purpose flour, spooned and leveled

½ teaspoon baking powder

1 teaspoon baking soda

½ teaspoon kosher salt

1 cup (227g) unsalted butter, softened

1 cup (200g) granulated sugar

½ cup (105g) light brown sugar, packed

1 large egg, room temperature

1 egg yolk, room temperature

½ teaspoon peppermint extract

1 teaspoon vanilla extract

½ cup (85g) white chocolate chips

Crushed peppermint, for topping

FOR THE FROSTING

1 cup (170g) white chocolate chips

1 cup (226g) unsalted butter, softened

4 ounces (113g) cream cheese, softened

2 cups (240g) powdered sugar

1-3 tablespoons heavy cream

1 teaspoon vanilla extract

½ teaspoon peppermint extract

⅛ teaspoon kosher salt

1 In a medium bowl, whisk together the all-purpose flour, baking powder, baking soda, and salt. Set this aside. In a large mixing bowl beat together the softened butter, granulated sugar, and brown sugar on high until light and fluffy. About two minutes. Add the egg, egg yolk, peppermint and vanilla and mix on medium until combined. Sprinkle in the dry ingredients and mix on low until just combined. Using a rubber spatula, fold in the white chocolate chips. Cover the dough and chill for 30 minutes. During the last 15 minutes of chill time, preheat the oven to 350°F (175°C) and line two baking sheets with parchment paper. Scoop our 3 tbsp sized cookie dough balls, roll them in your hands to form perfect circles, and place on the prepared baking sheets. Bake for 9-11 minutes and allow to fully cool while you make the white chocolate peppermint buttercream.

2 Make the buttercream by adding the white chocolate chips to a microwave safe bowl. Microwave for 30 second increments, stirring in between, until smooth. Allow the white chocolate to cool. In a mixing bowl, beat the softened butter and cream cheese on high until smooth. About 2-3 minutes. Reduce the speed to low, and add in the powdered sugar ½ cup at a time until fully mixed in. Add in the cooled white chocolate, 1 tbsp of heavy cream, vanilla, peppermint, and salt. Mix on medium until combined. If needed, add 1-2 more tbsp of heavy cream to achieve your desired consistency. Beat the buttercream on high for 1 minute until fluffy. Transfer the buttercream to a piping bag fitted with a decorative tip. Frost the cookies, top with crushed peppermint, and serve!

ITALIAN RAINBOW COOKIES

MAKES 30 1-INCH RAINBOW COOKIES

Every time I visit my sister in New York City, it starts and ends the same way, eating as many Italian rainbow cookies as we can! Rainbow cookies are layers of moist almond cake, with raspberry jam in between each layer, and then smothered with a thick layer of melted chocolate on top. Is there anything more delicious than that? While these cookies are a labor of love to make, you can make them! This recipe is fool proof and worth the extra love and time in the kitchen. These rainbow cookies are the perfect treat to gift around the holiday season in your Christmas cookie boxes!

FOR THE COOKIES

4 large eggs, separated, room temperature

1 cup (200g) granulated sugar

1½ teaspoons almond extract

1 teaspoon vanilla extract

8 ounces marzipan, cut into pieces

1½ cups (340g or 3 sticks) unsalted butter, softened

2 cups (240g) all-purpose flour, spooned and leveled

¼ teaspoon kosher salt

1-3 teaspoons red gel food coloring

1-3 teaspoons green gel food coloring

FOR THE FILLING AND TOPPING

1 cup (320g) raspberry jam, warmed

1 cup (170g) semisweet chocolate, melted

1 Preheat the oven to 350°F (175°C) and spray 3 9x9 baking dishes with cooking spray or butter. Line the dishes with parchment paper, leaving a little overhang. In a large mixing bowl, beat together the egg yolks, granulated sugar, almond extract, and vanilla extract until pale yellow and smooth. Set this aside. In another mixing bowl, beat the egg whites until soft peaks form. Be careful not to overbeat the egg whites. Set this aside. In a small bowl, heat the marzipan for 15-20 seconds until it is soft. Add this to a large mixing bowl with the butter. Cream the marzipan and butter together until smooth and creamy. Using a rubber spatula, fold in the egg yolk mixture into the almond paste mixture until well combined. Slowly sift in the flour and salt and mix until just combined, scraping down the sides of the bowl as needed. Fold in the egg whites until the batter is completely smooth.

2 In 3 clean bowls, divide the batter into three equal portions (about 330g each). Add the red food coloring to one bowl, the green to a second bowl, and leave the third bowl white. Mix until your desired shade of red and green are achieved. Spread the 3 batters into the 3 prepared baking dishes in an even layer. Bake for 10-12 minutes or until the edges are lightly golden and a toothpick inserted into the center comes out clean. Allow the cake layers to cool completely.

3 Heat the raspberry jam in the microwave for 30 seconds. Spread half of the raspberry jam over the green layer. Invert the white layer on top of the raspberry jam green layer. Spead the remaining jam on top of the white layer. Invert the red layer on top of the jam covered white layer and press down. Cover the layers tightly with plastic wrap and cover with a heavy cutting board or object. Place the rainbow cookies in the fridge to set for 3 hours or overnight. Once the rainbow cookies are fully chilled, remove them from the fridge.

4 Add the chocolate chips to a microwave safe bowl, and heat at 30 second increments stirring in between until fully melted and smooth. Pour the chocolate over the top of the red layer and spread it smooth and even over the whole cake. You can create beautiful waves in the chocolate using a fork or keep it smooth. Place the cake back in the fridge to allow the chocolate to set for 30 minutes. Once the chocolate is set, cut the rainbow cookies into small 1-inch squares to serve or gift to family and friends.

SOFT AND CHEWY CUT OUT GINGERBREAD

MAKES 14 MEDIUM GINGERBREAD

There is nothing that gets me in the Christmas spirit more than a warm, fresh baked batch of gingerbread cookies to decorate while I wrap presents with my family! It's tradition that every year we have a gingerbread baking and decorating night with the fire lit while Christmas songs fill the air. As warm spices of cinnamon, ginger, and sweet molasses fill the home, the kitchen begins to smell like Christmas itself. These soft and chewy gingerbread cookies are unlike your typical dry and crunchy gingerbread. They even have a secret ingredient that I'm sharing just with you. The orange zest blends perfectly with the warm spices adding a delicious layer to this traditional gingerbread.

2¼ cups (300g) all-purpose flour, spooned and leveled

¼ teaspoon kosher salt

2½ teaspoons ground ginger

2½ teaspoons ground cinnamon

½ teaspoon allspice

¼ teaspoon ground clove

¼ teaspoon nutmeg

6 tablespoons (85g) unsalted butter, softened

¾ cup (160g) light brown sugar, packed

2 tablespoons (25g) granulated sugar

1 teaspoon vanilla extract

2 tablespoons heavy cream (or milk)

½ teaspoon orange zest

2/3 cup (180g) molasses

1   In a medium bowl, whisk together the all-purpose flour, salt, ginger, cinnamon, allspice, clove, and nutmeg. Set this aside.

2   In a large mixing bowl, beat the softened butter, brown sugar, and granulated sugar together until light and fluffy, about 2-3 minutes. Mix in the vanilla extract and heavy cream. Add in the orange zest. Then, gradually add the molasses, mixing until everything is fully incorporated. Slowly add the dry ingredients to the wet mixture and mix until just combined. Wrap the dough in plastic wrap and refrigerate for at least 2 hours or overnight.

3   Preheat the oven to 350°F (175°C) and line two baking sheets with parchment paper. Remove the chilled dough from the refrigerator and place on a lightly floured work surface. Roll the dough out to about ¼ inch thick and use cookie cutters to cut out the cookies. When you run out of space, re-roll the dough and keep cutting out shapes until the dough is gone. Place the cookies on the prepared baking sheet. Bake the cookies for 8-10 minutes, until the edges are just set. Cool on the baking sheet for a few minutes, then transfer to a wire rack to cool completely. Frost using the Royal Icing recipe found on page 35.

SUGAR COOKIE CHRISTMAS TREES

MAKES 8 CHRISTMAS TREES

Mini Sugar Cookie Christmas Trees are a joyful addition to any holiday celebration! These soft and buttery cookies are shaped like little Christmas trees and decorated with bright green frosting and colorful sprinkles that make them look extra festive. They're perfect for cookie decorating with the kids or simply enjoying while cozied up with loved ones. Each bite is a delightful reminder of the magic of the season, making these mini trees a sweet treat to share, gift, or enjoy at your holiday gatherings.

FOR THE COOKIES

2¾ cups (330g) all-purpose flour, spooned and leveled

1 teaspoon baking soda

½ teaspoon baking powder

½ teaspoon kosher salt

1 cup (227g) unsalted butter, softened

1 cup (200g) granulated sugar

½ cup (105g) light brown sugar, packed

1 large egg, room temperature

1 egg yolk, room temperature

1½ teaspoons almond extract

1 teaspoon vanilla extract

FOR THE FROSTING

½ cup (113g) unsalted butter, at room temperature

2½ cups (300g) powdered sugar

½ teaspoon vanilla extract

1-3 tablespoons heavy cream

1-3 drops green gel food coloring

¼ teaspoon kosher salt

Sprinkles for decorating

1 Whisk together the all-purpose flour, baking soda, baking powder, and salt in a bowl and set it aside. In a large bowl, beat together the butter, granulated sugar, and brown sugar until it's light and fluffy, about 2 minutes. Add in the egg and egg yolk one at a time until fully incorporated. Add in the almond extract and vanilla to the butter mixture and beat until it's light and fluffy. Slowly add in the dry ingredients until a dough forms. Do not overmix. Allow the dough to chill in the fridge for 30 minutes. During the last 15 minutes of chill time, preheat the oven to 350°F (175°C) and line two baking sheets with parchment paper.

2 Using a 1, 2, and 3 tablespoon sized cookie dough scoop, scoop out different sized cookie dough balls until the dough is gone and place them on the prepared baking sheets. Bake the 1 tablespoon sized cookie dough for 5-7 minutes, 2 tablespoon sized cookie dough for 6-8 minutes and 3 tablespoon sized cookie dough for 9-11 minutes. Let the cookies cool on the baking sheet before transferring them to a cooling rack.

3 While the cookies cool, make the buttercream by beating the butter on high until smooth and creamy for about 3-4 minutes. Add in the powdered sugar ½ cup at a time and beat on low, slowly increasing the speed until fully combined. Add in the vanilla extract, 1 tablespoon heavy cream, green gel food coloring, and salt mixing until incorporated. If needed, add in 1-2 more tbsp heavy cream to achieve your desired consistency. Transfer the buttercream to a piping bag fitted with a decorative tip.

4 Assemble the Christmas trees by piping a layer of buttercream on top of the largest sugar cookie, place the second largest on top of the frosting, pipe an even layer of buttercream, and top with the smallest cookie. Frost the top of the tree and add sprinkles.

CHOCOLATE CANDY CANE COOKIES

MAKES 10 COOKIES

Every year during the holiday season, we get in our Christmas pajamas, make mugs full of warm hot cocoa topped with whipped cream, listen to holiday songs, and drive around and look at the beautiful Christmas lights. We always make sure to pack a few Christmas cookies for the holiday drive to dip in our cocoa. These chocolate candy cane cookies have a rich chocolate base that is perfectly soft and chewy. Then topped with a thick layer of peppermint candy cane buttercream, this is the ultimate holiday cookie. Bake up a batch and enjoy them by the fire or looking at Christmas lights.

FOR THE COOKIES

1 cup (120g) all-purpose flour, spooned and leveled

2/3 cup (56g) Dutch processed cocoa powder

1 teaspoon baking soda

⅛ teaspoon kosher salt

½ cup (113g) unsalted butter, softened

½ cup (100g) granulated sugar

½ cup (105g) light brown sugar, packed

1 large egg, room temperature

1 teaspoon vanilla extract

1 teaspoon peppermint extract

1 tablespoon milk

1 cup (170g) semi-sweet chocolate chips

FOR THE FROSTING

½ cup (113g) unsalted butter, softened

2½ cups (300g) powdered sugar

2-3 tablespoons heavy cream

1 teaspoon vanilla extract

½ teaspoon peppermint extract

1-4 drops red food coloring

¼ cup Crushed peppermint candy canes for topping

1. Preheat the oven to 350°F (175°C) and line two baking sheets with parchment paper. In a bowl, whisk together the all-purpose flour, cocoa powder, baking soda, and salt. Set aside. In a large mixing bowl, beat together the unsalted butter, granulated sugar, and light brown sugar until light and fluffy, about 2 minutes. Add in the egg, vanilla, and peppermint extract and mix until combined. Sprinkle in the dry ingredients and mix until just combined. Add in the milk and chocolate chips and beat on high for 1 minute.

2. Using a 3-tablespoon sized cookie dough scoop, scoop out the cookie dough and place it on the prepared baking sheet. Bake for 9-11 minutes until the edges are starting to set. The middle will look underdone, it will set as it cools. Allow to cool completely before serving.

3. Meanwhile, prepare the peppermint buttercream. In a large bowl, beat the softened butter until light and fluffy, about 3-4 minutes. Add in the powdered sugar and mix on low slowly increasing the speed until combined. Add in 1 tablespoon of heavy cream, vanilla extract, peppermint extract, and red food coloring. I like to use 1 drop for a light pink peppermint color and mix until combined. Add in 1-2 more tablespoons heavy cream to achieve your desired consistency. Spread the peppermint buttercream on half of each cookie and sprinkle with crushed peppermints.

FROSTED SPARKLING CRANBERRY SUGAR COOKIES

MAKES 12 COOKIES

These chewy, frosted sugar cookies are topped with sparkly, sugared cranberries that are sure to get you in the holiday spirit. These sugared cranberries are the perfect balance of tart and sweet, and look beautiful atop the smooth white buttercream. Each sugar cookie is studded with chewy cranberries making these the ultimate holiday treat.

FOR THE CRANBERRIES

⅓ cup (79g) water

1 cup (200g) granulated sugar, divided

1 cup (100g) fresh cranberries, rinsed and dried

Rosemarry sprigs for topping, if desired

FOR THE COOKIES

2¾ cups (330g) all-purpose flour, spooned and leveled

1 teaspoon baking soda

½ teaspoon baking powder

½ teaspoon kosher salt

1 cup (227g) unsalted butter, softened

1 cup (200g) granulated sugar, plus ½ cup (100g) more for rolling

½ cup (105g) light brown sugar, packed

1 large egg, room temperature

1 egg yolk, room temperature

1½ teaspoons almond extract

1 teaspoon vanilla extract

1 cup dried cranberries

FOR THE BUTTERCREAM

1 cup (226g) unsalted butter, softened

2 cups (240g) powdered sugar

1-3 tablespoons heavy cream

1 teaspoon vanilla extract

⅛ teaspoon kosher salt

1 Start by making the sugared, sparkling cranberries. In a medium saucepan, combine ⅓ cup water and ½ cup sugar. Bring to a boil and let it simmer on low heat for 2-3 minutes. Stir in the cranberries to fully coat in the syrup. Remove the saucepan from the heat and continue stirring for 1 minute. Remove the cranberries with a slotted spoon and transfer to a parchment lined baking sheet or a metal rack to let cranberries dry while you make the cookies.

2 Make the cookies. In a medium bowl, whisk the flour, baking soda, baking powder, and salt in a bowl and set it aside. In a large mixing bowl, beat together the butter, granulated sugar, and brown sugar until it is light and fluffy, about 2 minutes. Add the egg and egg yolk one at a time until fully incorporated. Add in the almond extract and vanilla to the butter mixture, beat until it's light and fluffy. Slowly add the dry ingredients until a dough forms. Do not overmix. Using a rubber spatula, fold in the dried cranberries. Allow the dough to chill in the fridge for 30 minutes.

3 While the dough chills, make the buttercream. In a mixing bowl, beat the butter on high until it is light and smooth, about 2 minutes. Reduce the speed and add in the powdered sugar ½ cup at a time until combined. Add in 1 tbsp heavy cream and vanilla extract mixing on medium speed until smooth. If needed, add in 1-2 more tbsp of heavy cream to achieve your desired consistency. Add in the salt and beat on high for 1 minute until fluffy. Transfer the buttercream to a piping bag fitted with a piping tip.

4 During the last 15 minutes of chill time, preheat the oven to 350°F (175°C) and line two baking sheets with parchment paper. Using a 3 tbsp sized cookie dough scoop, scoop out the cookie dough balls, place them on the baking sheets, and bake for 9-11 minutes. Finish making the sugared cranberries by rolling them in batches in the remaining ½ cup of sugar to coat them. Assemble the cookies by piping an even layer of buttercream over each cookie. Top the buttercream with a few sugared, sparkling cranberries and sprig of rosemary.

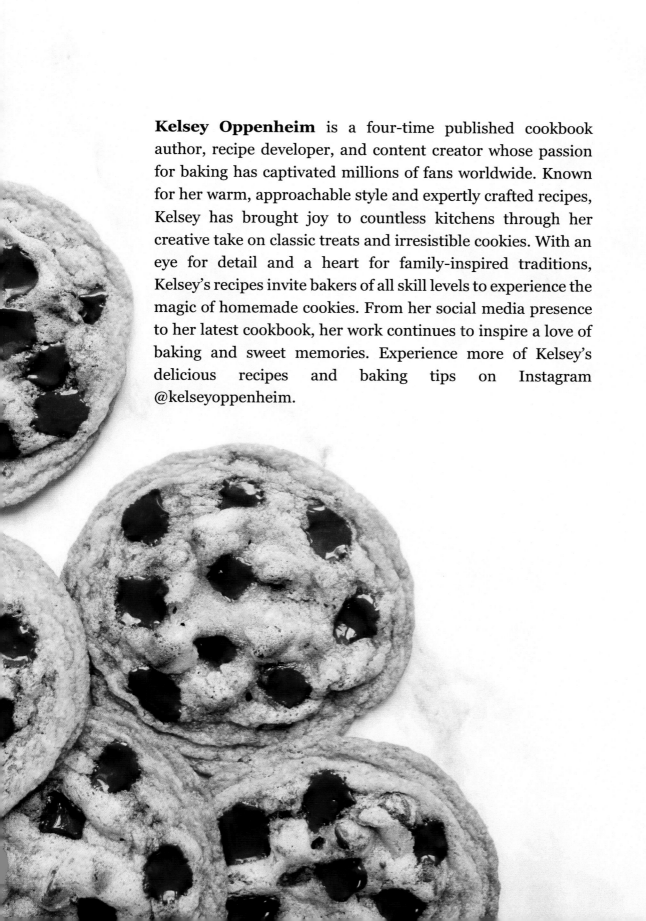

Kelsey Oppenheim is a four-time published cookbook author, recipe developer, and content creator whose passion for baking has captivated millions of fans worldwide. Known for her warm, approachable style and expertly crafted recipes, Kelsey has brought joy to countless kitchens through her creative take on classic treats and irresistible cookies. With an eye for detail and a heart for family-inspired traditions, Kelsey's recipes invite bakers of all skill levels to experience the magic of homemade cookies. From her social media presence to her latest cookbook, her work continues to inspire a love of baking and sweet memories. Experience more of Kelsey's delicious recipes and baking tips on Instagram @kelseyoppenheim.